TOWARD A MATURE FAITH: DOES BIBLICAL INERRANCY MAKE SENSE?

Clayton Sullivan

SBC TODAY   DECATUR

First Printing, September 1990
Second Printing, November 1990

Library of Congress Catalog Card Number: 90-091988

ISBN 0-9627617-0-2

Published by
SBC TODAY
222 East Lake Drive
Decatur, Georgia 30030
1990

❦

Christians, it is needless to say, utterly detest each other.
They slander each other constantly with the vilest forms of abuse and
cannot come to any sort of agreement in their teaching.
Each sect brands its own, fills the head of its own with deceitful nonsense,
and makes perfect little pigs of those it wins over to its side.
Celsus
On the True Doctrine

❦

What are the limits of tolerance?
Does not tolerance of a theological position which one knows or
believes to be untrue become a betrayal of the truth?
Reinhold Niebuhr
Leaves from the Notebooks of a Tamed Cynic

❦

Religion is the only field of human inquiry
where a premium is placed upon intellectual dishonesty.
Albert Schweitzer

❦

Father, forgive them, for they know not what they do.
Jesus of Nazareth

CONTENTS

❦

PREFACE

❦

Books should not be written in and for a vacuum. Instead, every book should be authored to meet a reader's need and to correlate with a reader's interest. In order, therefore, is the question: *for whom* and *why* was this book written?

Toward a Mature Faith: Does Biblical Inerrancy Make Sense? has not been written for biblical scholars or for seminary-trained pastors. Seminary teachers, university religion professors, and ministers who have graduated from mainline seminaries will find nothing "new" on the pages which follow. Ideas advanced, arguments developed, and information explored in this book will be familiar to them.

Instead, *Toward a Mature Faith: Does Biblical Inerrancy Make Sense?* has been written, first of all, *for the laity.* I am writing for "in-the-pew" church members (housewives, attorneys, nurses, school teachers, accountants) who have inquisitive minds and who have a desire to understand the Bible in a responsible way. Secondly, this book has been written *for college students* and *for seminarians* who are neophytes as far as biblical studies are concerned. My hope is that the discussion which follows will help them find their way through the interpretive "mine field" which surrounds the Bible in some quarters today.

This book's purpose is to grapple with the question: is the biblical inerrancy theory plausible? Does inerrancy make sense? In broaching this issue I do not have in mind complex, equivocal versions of inerrancy subscribed to by scholars like James I. Packer. Instead, this book focuses on the "popular" or "folk" version of inerrancy. By "popular" I mean biblical inerrancy as understood by "the folks"—by scores of believers who Sunday by Sunday attend Bible classes, participate in worship services, and support the church with their money.

This popular version of inerrancy has been around for approximately a century. Originally it was hammered out on the eastern seaboard by Princeton theologians like Charles Hodge and Benjamin B. Warfield. In his *Systematic Theology*, for example, Charles Hodge asserted that the Bible's moral and religious truths and its statements of facts ("whether scientific, historical, or geographical") are all inspired. This assertion, I suggest, gets to the heart of the folk-version of inerrancy. "The Bible is void of errors, contradictions, or problematic passages. Every statement found therein is valid and is believable to modern man." As one inerrantist spokesman recently asserted, the Bible is "the flawless epitome of impeccable perfection to the minutest, microscopic detail." On pages which follow I will ponder this stance.

This book does not have the format I originally intended. At first, I projected a book with multiple authors. I wanted it to contain essays by both inerrantists and non-inerrantists, and I wanted these essays to be based upon evidence derived from biblical texts. In other words, my first intention was for this book to be a dialogue or a debate in which cases for and against inerrancy would be presented, evaluated, and answered. These cases were to be based upon the phenomena of biblical texts ("what the Bible says"), not upon opinions concerning biblical inerrancy. This give-and-take approach, I believe, would have been illuminating. I regret to state that (despite many letters written and a fortune spent on long-distance telephone calls) I could not locate recognized inerrantist spokesmen willing to join in such a debate. Consequently, this book has necessarily assumed its present form.

Readers may inquire: why go to the trouble of asking if inerrancy makes sense? Broaching questions, I believe, can clarify our thinking and can deliver us from half-truths. Questions have a capacity to liberate from false views which are used to manipulate the naive, the uninformed, the credulous. Moreover, the posing of questions can lead to right understanding. As Pierre Abelard, medieval theologian, remarked in the prologue to his *Sic et Non*, "The first key to wisdom is constant and frequent questions. By doubting we are led to question and by questioning we arrive at the truth."

I have worked on this book sporadically for over three years. During this time it has undergone numerous revisions. I express gratitude to the following persons who read this book in earlier versions and who made invaluable suggestions: Dr. Glen Pearson (a physician with an amazing knowledge of English grammar), Eunice McSwain (community-college teacher), Edd Rowell (editor), Dr. Frank Stagg (seminary professor), Tony Bernard (ministerial student), Alan Perry (an attorney who taught me how to spell correctly the name of John Stuart Mill), Janet Purvis (housewife), Warren Dale (chemical engineer), Dick Conville (university professor) and Hugh Dickens (educator).

Finally, I express gratitude to Charla Bullard and to Henry Goodwin of The University of Southern Mississippi's Publication and Printing Services; their artistic and editorial expertise (as well as their patience) made this book possible.

Clayton Sullivan
Department of Philosophy and Religion
The University of Southern Mississippi

CHAPTER ONE

❦

The Inerrancy Controversy

*A*s far as religious controversies are concerned, our century has not been a peaceful one; to the contrary, doctrinal and moral disputes have abounded within the church. Christians have disagreed over clerical celibacy, abortion, draft resistance, papal infallibility, prayer in public schools, artificial birth control, female ordination, tax funds for parochial schools, and the teaching of creationism. They have argued over hymnody and liturgy revisions. They have not always seen eye to eye on civil rights issues. The subjects for dispute have been legion.

This discussion will focus upon still another issue which has vexed the church, and that issue is *biblical inerrancy*—a doctrine over which white-hot controversy has periodically erupted throughout this century. The inerrancy issue disturbed the Presbyterian and Methodist Churches back in the early 1900s. Later on in the 1960s and 1970s the Missouri Synod dispute occurred within the Lutheran Church. Today an inerrancy debate is boiling within the Southern Baptist Convention, this country's largest Protestant denomination. In these controversies churches have been damaged, charges have been exchanged, and ecclesiastical careers have been marred. Our task on the pages which follow will be "to explain" this inerrancy dispute. Where is the battlefield, who are the warriors, what are the issues?

Regardless of one's personal view, candor compels the assertion that across the years (particularly since the turn of the century) rank-and-file Christians by the thousands have believed in biblical inerrancy. As inerrantists they contend that *every statement* found in the Bible is figuratively or factually or historically true. One of the reasons they hold this belief is that time and again they have heard recognized spokesmen for the Christian faith advocate and defend biblical inerrancy. This development is not novel; a common means by which we acquire many of our beliefs (whether in medicine or politics or economics or religion) is by heeding acknowledged leaders in these fields—especially leaders whom we admire. No person can be skilled in all areas. Aware of our limitations, we tend to accept at face value what respected, authoritative persons tell us (particularly when we have no expertise in the area under consideration).

A recognition that we acquire beliefs by heeding authorities helps us to understand (at least in part) why biblical inerrancy has become a viewpoint widely and devoutly held in some parts of the church. For decades charismatic clergymen have proclaimed biblical inerrancy. Repeatedly they have expressed to parishioners the view that the Bible is a book void of limitations, mistakes, contradictions, or puzzles. To support this position they have quoted II Timothy 3:16 which asserts (in the King James version): "All scripture is given by inspiration of God, and is profitable for doctrine, for reproof, for correction, for instruction in righteousness." Believing what they are told, well-intentioned Christians have come to view biblical inerrancy as a vital component of the Christian faith.

Raised in the Deep South, I—as a youngster—lived in a religio-social setting where this belief in biblical inerrancy was universally accepted. The Bible's "content" or "message" was never questioned. A frequently-quoted proverb was: "If the Bible says it, that settles it!" Indeed, the Bible itself was an object of veneration. From my youth I have memories of congregations rising to their feet when the Bible was read during worship services. During these services clergymen delivered exegetical sermons which were "straight out of the Bible." Church members took pride in owning elegant Bibles which were printed on high-quality paper, bound in leather covers, and embossed with gold. During the week they displayed these Bibles in their homes, and on Sunday they carried them to church services. Veneration for the Bible was reflected in the hymns we sang, and words from those hymns still live in my mind.

Holy Bible, book divine,
Precious treasure, thou art mine;
Mine to tell me whence I came;
Mine to tell me what I am.

Religious empathy and a sense of good taste compel the assertion that Bible veneration (as a religious practice) and biblical inerrancy (as a belief) ought to be respected. Devotion to the principle of religious liberty compels the assertion that Christians have a right to believe in biblical inerrancy and to venerate the Bible as though it were an icon. Over the years this belief and practice have provided scores of believers with a frame-of-reference from which to understand their faith. Moreover, Bible veneration and the belief in biblical inerrancy ought never be ridiculed. *That which is sacred and meaningful to some should never be treated with contempt by others.*

But even as candor compels the recognition that many Christians subscribe to biblical inerrancy, candor also compels the assertion that others do not. To them inerrancy does *not* "make sense." They are aware that "biblical inerrancy" is a phrase of recent vintage. And they are aware that this phrase would never have entered the church's vocabulary had there not emerged in the eighteenth and nineteenth centuries a new method of biblical study which today is known as the *historical- critical method.* At the core of this method was a mutation (a new development) in biblical studies. This mutation can be stated succinctly: scholars for the first time began studying the Bible as they study other works of literature. When, for example, scholars study Shakespeare's plays, they ask probing questions such as: in what order were the plays written? How does *Hamlet's* structure compare to the structure of *The Merchant of Venice?* Was Shakespeare anti-Semitic? What "message" or commentary on life is conveyed in *Macbeth?* How were the tragedies staged in the Globe theatre? Shakespearean students make every effort to interpret and to understand the plays in the context of sixteenth-and-seventeenth century English society.

During the eighteenth century scholars began using a similar technique while studying the Bible, and this technique (as I have previously observed) came to be known as the *historical-critical method*—a phrase which is puzzling. Particularly curious is the term *critical*—a word which suggests fault finding. Thus when some people hear about scholars studying the Bible "critically," they—quite understandably—conclude: "Scholars are 'picking' on the Bible. They are searching for faults." But we must remember that the word "critical" has another meaning besides censoriousness. Derived from a Greek root which means "to discern," it also can convey the idea of being *careful, discriminating, exacting.* In this sense we sometimes remark about a person, "He has a cautious, *critical* mind." Or someone remarks, "I need to weigh *critically* all the factors involved before I reach a decision." Or, "We should read newspapers with a *critical eye.*" In these statements "critical" and "critically" have nothing to do with fault finding; instead, they have a connotation of cautiousness. It is in this reflective, cautious sense that "critical" is used in the phrase "historical-critical method." To study the Bible with this method means to examine carefully its books against their historical background (giving attention to when, where, and under what circumstances they were written) and to study them inquisitively as to their text, composition, and character. In other words, the historical-critical method involves the reverent, systematic application of the mind's evaluative and analytical capacities to the books of the Bible.

Numerous scholars in the nineteenth century dedicated their professional lives to a historical- critical study of the Bible. One of my favorites is Constantin von Tischendorf (1815-1874), a German scholar of astonishing physical vitality. While a student at the University of Leipzig, he developed an interest in the Greek New Testament. Studying the Greek New Testament in meticulous detail became his life's consuming passion.

To this end Tischendorf made numerous trips to the Middle East in quest of early Greek manuscripts of the New Testament. Time and again he visited the Monastery of St. Catherine on the Sinai Peninsula. This Greek Orthodox monastery, built at the traditional site of the burning bush, was founded in 527 by the Roman emperor Justinian.

A pilgrimage center during the Middle Ages, the monastery —with its gray, granite walls—still retains much of its original appearance. Tischendorf repeatedly visited St. Catherine's; he did so in order to avail himself of the monastery's library which contained a treasure of manuscripts, some of them the oldest in the church's possession.

During an 1859 visit Tischendorf was shown (by the monastery's cook!) a Greek manuscript of the Bible which (scholars now believe) was written possibly in the latter half of the fourth century. Containing most of the Old Testament, the entire New Testament, and two early Christian works named the *Letter of Barnabas* and the *Shepherd of Hermas*, this incredibly old and valued manuscript is known as *Codex Sinaiticus*. Housed for a time in Moscow, it is now in the British Museum in London. The recovery of this manuscript by Tischendorf has made possible the reconstructing of a more accurate text of the Greek New Testament. For example, Mark's gospel in *Codex Sinaiticus* ends with Mark 16:8; the last twelve verses (Mark 16:9 to 16:20) are not present. Scholars have discovered that these last twelve verses do not appear in other early Greek manuscripts of the New Testament; instead, they appear only in later Greek manuscripts. Evidently these verses, which contain references to drinking poison and to handling snakes as evidence of Christian faith, were added to Mark's gospel by an unknown Christian scribe. Thanks to the energy and curiosity of scholars like Tischendorf, we now know these twelve verses were not originally a part of Mark's gospel. Reconstructing an accurate text of the books in the Bible has been one of the major enterprises of historical-critical studies.

The historical-critical method, however, was not concerned solely with the reconstruction of accurate biblical texts. Students of this method had an equal interest in *interpretation*. How should various biblical passages be *understood*? What message or significance could be found in them? An interest in interpretation was unavoidable as scholars became aware of the Bible's complexity. For the Bible contains various types of literature: allegories, parables, psalms, poetry, proverbs, historical accounts, confessions of faith, gospels, prophetic pronouncements, letters, wisdom literature, law codes, apocalyptic and pseudonymous works.

As scholars become aware of this complexity, they encountered interpretive puzzles. As an example of an interpretive puzzle I will cite the gospel of John. John, commonly referred to as the Fourth Gospel, presents an account of Jesus' life which–in many ways–is different from the account found in Matthew, Mark, and Luke. Consider, for instance, the matter of parables. Many people find it impossible to think of Jesus without thinking of him as a parable-teller. Who has not heard of the parable of the Good Samaritan or the Prodigal Son? Indeed, Matthew goes so far as to assert that Jesus said nothing without a parable (Matthew 13:34). Yet a reading of the Fourth Gospel, a gospel containing numerous discourses spoken by Jesus, reveals that it contains *no parables.* This total absence of parables is a striking feature of John's gospel. But this absence broaches a question: if it be true that Jesus did not speak without using parables (as Matthew 13:34 observes), then why are his discourses in the Fourth Gospel void of parables?

Moreover, in the first three gospels (Matthew, Mark, and Luke) Jesus is presented time and again as an exorcist–one who casts out demons. Reflective New Testament students found themselves perplexed on discovering that John's gospel is completely lacking in demon exorcisms. But neither, scholars discovered, does the Fourth Gospel contain accounts of Jesus' baptism, his wilderness temptation, his association with outcasts and sinners, his transfiguration, his institution of the Eucharist, his Gethsemane agony, or his dereliction cry.

Additionally, the Fourth Gospel contains episodes not mentioned in the first three gospels: the turning of water into wine at Cana, the healing of the impotent man at Bethesda, the giving of sight at Siloam to the man born blind, and the raising of Lazarus from the dead. Also distinctive to the Fourth Gospel are the prolonged conversations with Nicodemus and with the Samaritan woman, the advice given to Jesus by his brothers to go up to Jerusalem to win disciples at the feast, the visit of the Greeks, the feet-washing scene, the judicial appearance before Annas, the visit of Peter and the other disciple to the empty tomb, and the conviction of "doubting" Thomas.

The point is: historical-critical scholars came to recognize that the account of Jesus' life presented in the Fourth Gospel is different from the account presented in Matthew, Mark, and Luke. To express the matter another way, the Jesus encountered in John's gospel is not identical with the Jesus presented in the first three gospels. This difference provokes an interpretive question. How far is it possible for us to use the Fourth Gospel as a dependable witness to the life and teachings of Jesus? In John's gospel do we have a "photograph" of Jesus, or do we have a "portrait" of Jesus–a portrait painted by an early Christian thinker who presented Jesus in terms meaningful to the Greek and Roman world of the first century?

Many Christians welcomed this historical-critical method which scholars[1] developed–a method which recognized and grappled with interpretive issues. To them it was a breath of fresh air. But others resented the historical-critical method. They feared its conclusions. For example, they disliked the suggestions that the Noah flood account in Genesis is patterned after a Mesopotamian flood story which we read about in the *Gilgamesh Epic* [2] and that the Genesis creation account is fashioned after the Mesopotamian creation story found in the *Enuma Elish.*[3] They were apprehensive about the theory that Isaiah's prophecy did not come from one mind but was instead a composite work coming from widely-different periods in Jewish history.[4]

This fear of and resentment toward the historical-critical method was one factor (but not the only factor) which led to the emergence within the church of a movement known as *fundamentalism.*[5] This movement, appearing in the North around the turn of the century, was led by evangelicals like J. Gresham Machen, Benjamin B. Warfield, and Rueben Torry. A prominent feature of the fundamentalist movement was the holding of Bible conferences. These conferences were both religious and recreational in nature.

At one of these conferences—the 1895 Niagara Bible Conference in New York—a resolution was issued which listed five beliefs which were judged by evangelicals to be essential to the Christian faith. Those five points were: (1) the inerrancy of the Scriptures, (2) Jesus' virgin birth, (3) substitutionary atonement, (4) Jesus' physical resurrection, and (5) his bodily return to earth. A similar statement was approved in 1910 by the General Assembly of the Northern Presbyterian Church. The custom emerged of referring to these five core beliefs as "fundamentals" of the Christian religion. Thus *fundamentalism*[6] is a movement devoted to propagating what some perceive to be the *fundamentals (core beliefs)* of the Christian faith, and participants in this movement are labeled *fundamentalists.*

Of particular interest to us is the fundamental known as *biblical inerrancy,* a phrase which did not enter the church's vocabulary until the turn of the century. This fundamental contends that the Bible is free of mistakes, inconsistencies, and contradictions. On all topics it is morally, historically, and scientifically correct. Having adopted this "accuracy" presupposition, fundamentalists began fighting battles on behalf of inerrancy. They wrote books in which the historical-critical method was criticized. Condemning sermons were preached. Seminary professors who were supportive of the historical-critical method and who did not subscribe to inerrancy were subjected to heresy trials. "Liberal" clergymen like Harry Emerson Fosdick, the Manhattan minister, were lampooned.

These inerrancy battles, occurring during this century's opening decades, were fought mainly in the North. Denominations located in this country's interior—like the Lutheran and Southern Baptist—were largely untouched by the inerrancy controversy of the early 1900s. Neither Lutherans (isolated in the Midwest) nor Southern Baptists (isolated in the South, which economically was flat on its back in the lingering aftermath of the Civil War) had extensive exposure to the historical-critical method.

Churches in our country's interior would possibly have continued to be unexposed to the historical-critical method had it not been for that sociological Armageddon called the Second World War. This sociological Armageddon's impact can be illustrated by noting what happened among Southern Baptists. Prior to the Second World War Southern Baptists existed in an insulated, agrarian culture. Their world was a bucolic South of one-horse farmers, one-crop agriculture, one-party politics, and one-room schools. Stretching from Texas to the Carolinas and Virginia, this agrarian South, portrayed in the novels of Erskine Caldwell and William Faulkner, was a montage of weather-beaten barns plastered with Prince Albert tobacco signs, gullied hills, mules and plows, and postage-stamp-size towns bearing quaint names like Log Cabin and Hot Coffee. People were poor; in vast areas industry was non-existent. Seven of every ten Southerners lived either on farms or in small towns.

But during the 1940s, decade of the Second World War, the South experienced a sociological and cultural fruit-basket-turn-over. Southerners by the tens of thousands were ripped off farms and out of small towns and were sent around the world as soldiers (their mental horizons thereby forever altered). Industry came south, the Negro went north, and cotton culture exited to California and Brazil. Farmers moved to cities to become factory workers, and diesel tractors replaced the mule and plough. Television arrived, and the county fair went the way of all flesh. Cow colleges became state universities, and Southerners (who had always been told what to believe by politicians, preachers, and newspaper editors) started thinking for themselves.

Among Southerners who started thinking for themselves were Southern Baptist clergymen. Instead of attending exclusively Baptist institutions of higher learning, they "went off" to study at schools like Yale, Harvard, the University of Chicago, Tübingen, Oxford, and Edinburgh. At these schools they absorbed the historical-critical method which for decades had dominated schools and churches outside the South. Other Southern Baptist pastors and professors studied this method on their own. In other words, a minority of Southern Baptist ministers started breathing in a twentieth-century intellectual atmosphere, exposing themselves to thought-worlds other than the thought-world of the "Old Time Religion." The Southern Baptist Theological Seminary in Louisville, Kentucky, was the path-finder which led Southern Baptists into the twentieth-century intellectual world. From this Kentucky seminary the historical-critical method flowed to other Baptist colleges and seminaries and into Baptist pulpits. A similar move into a twentieth-century thought-world transpired in other denominations also.

Thus an impasse—a Mexican standoff—exists. Some mainline churches (the United Methodist Church, the Episcopal Church, the Presbyterian Church U.S.A.) have nothing to do with inerrancy—a position they rightly or wrongly view as intellectually bankrupt. Others (the Presbyterian Church in America, the "conservative" wing of the Missouri Synod of the Lutheran Church) accept inerrancy. Moreover, inerrantists are now seizing control of the Southern Baptist Convention, this country's largest denomination. Convinced of the rightness of their position, inerrantists believe that pastors, denominational workers, and seminary professors who do not subscribe to inerrancy should be banished. But is their banishment justifiable? Do non-inerrantists have a leg to stand on? Maybe they don't. And then again maybe they do. This is why I propose we now give attention to non-inerrantists and try to understand why they reason as they do. I want us to attempt to understand why the biblical inerrancy theory does not make sense to them.

❧

NOTES

[1]Representative scholars who could be cited are W. F. Albright, S. R. Driver, H. L. Ginsberg, Martin Noth, Johannes Pedersen, George Foot Moore, Johannes Weiss, and Julius Wellhausen. Julius Wellhausen (1844-1918) is the example *par excellence* of a scholar devoted to the historical-critical method. A German orientalist, he began his career as an Old Testament professor at the University of Greifswald and continued as a Semitist at the Universities of Halle, Marburg, and Göttingen. For years Wellhausen focused his mental energies on the Hebrew text of the first five books in the Old Testament (the Pentateuch or the Books of Moses). Continuing the research of German scholars like Karl Heinrich Graf and Wilhelm Vatke, he observed in these five biblical books numerous anachronisms, duplicate accounts, and variations in literary style. On the basis of these observations Wellhausen concluded that the Pentateuch (rather than being a literary unity produced by one author) is a fusing of several sourcesor traditions (traditionally designated by the letters J, E, D, and P).

[2]The *Gilgamesh Epic*, written in cuneiform on eleven clay tablets, was discovered in Asshurbanipal's library in the ruins of Nineveh. Much of the epic concerns the heroic expeditions of Gilgamesh and his companion Enkidu. The epic's central theme is death's inevitability. Tablet XI contains the story of Utnapishtim who (like Noah) built a boat, gathered animals into it, and survived a devastating flood. English translations of the *Gilgamesh Epic* are available. Particularly readable is *The Epic of Gilgamesh* translated by N. K. Sandars; published by Penguin Books, this translation is furnished with ten introductory essays dealing with such topics as the epic's discovery and its historical background.

[3]The *Enuma Elish* is the title given to the Mesopotamian creation story. Like the *Gilgamesh Epic*, it was written in cuneiform on clay tablets and was discovered in Asshurbanipal's palace in the ruins of Nineveh. The sequence of events in the *Enuma Elish* is similar to the sequence in Genesis 1.

[4]Chapters 1-39 of Isaiah presuppose an eighth-century B. C. background. Chapters 40-48 presuppose the Babylonian exile (sixth-century B. C.).

[5]Any person interested in exploring fundamentalism in depth ought to read George M. Marsden's *Fundamentalism and American Culture: The Shaping of Twentieth-Century Evangelicalism 1870-1925* (New York, 1980).

[6]Fundamentalism is not *just* a belief-system centering (in part) on inerrancy. Fundamentalism is also a *mood*, a *temper*, a *frame of mind*. One

element of this mood is anti-intellectualism. Another element is angry militancy. Many fundamentalists have a Damascus-Road complex which compels them "to go after" fellow Christians with whom they disagree and (if possible) to destroy them. George M. Marsden develops this insight in his article "Evangelical and Fundamental Christianity" on pp. 190-197 of Vol. 5 of *The Encyclopedia of Religion* published (1987) by the Macmillan Publishing Company, New York.

❧

CHAPTER TWO

Why Non-Inerrantists Reason As They Do

M any rank-and-file Christians, admittedly, view non-inerrantists and their commitment to the historical-critical method as an ecclesiastical cancer. Yet in this chapter I want us to scrutinize these non-inerrantists. Why do they think as they think? Are they a destructive fifth-column within the Christian faith? Or are they Christians of sincerity and goodwill who have been forced—as a result of biblical research—to shun inerrantism?

I think non-inerrantist seminary professors, pastors, and lay persons would begin a response to such questions by asserting: "We know many view us as a Trojan horse within the church. They charge we are heretics who are subverting the Christian faith. But this is not the way we view ourselves. We value the Bible and affirm its authority. As active churchmen we view the Bible as being indispensable for comprehending the Christian faith. Yet, as inquisitive Christians we have been influenced by what has happened in biblical studies over the past several decades. Beginning in the eighteenth century (the Enlightenment), the Bible has been subjected to detailed examination. The texts composing Holy Scripture have undergone microscopic study at the hands and minds of hundreds of scholars. Viewing study as a form of worship, they have scrutinized the Bible book by book, chapter by chapter, verse by verse, word by word, letter by letter. As a result of this investigation we know more today about the biblical texts than was known in previous periods of church history. We have at our disposal tools of study (biblical dictionaries and encyclopedias, photographic manuscript reproductions, commentaries, concordances, lexicons, grammars, atlases, monographs, printed texts of the Hebrew

Old Testament and the Greek New Testament furnished with textual apparatus, journals published by scholarly organizations like the Society of Biblical Literature) which were unavailable to Christians during the Middle Ages or the Reformation or the Colonial era. As a result of this explosion of biblical knowledge we have been driven to conclusions which we feel are demanded by the evidence. One of those conclusions is: the Bible has a *human side* and is not void of puzzles and errors. Thus we cannot view Holy Scripture as inerrantists do. They contend the Bible is *void of any* mistakes, contradictions, or conundrums. But their inerrancy claim we could not make without closing our eyes to contrary evidence and without separating ourselves from mainline Protestant and Roman Catholic scholarship."

So non-inerrantists within the church reason, and I am proposing we try to understand why they think as they do. A Bulgarian proverb contends that *in some circumstances* we are justified in walking briefly even with the devil himself. I propose we walk briefly with the non-inerrantists and attempt to comprehend their reasoning process. To do this I want us to look at five passages in the Bible which (at least to non-inerrantists) are puzzling. These passages, chosen arbitrarily, illustrate why they find it difficult to go along with the inerrantist contention that *every* statement in the Bible *can* (or must) be taken as *inerrant.* The passages we are about to consider deal with (1) the divine name (Yahweh), (2) King Jehoiachin's coronation age, (3) the molten sea in Solomon's temple, (4) Judas Iscariot's death following his disposal of the betrayal money, and (5) Paul's Damascus Road experience. I ask you—the reader—to read carefully the analyses of these passages which follow. *By all means read these passages in your own Bible.* As you study these five passages—and the analyses of them—ask yourself the question: Are non-inerrantists right or wrong in suggesting they contain puzzles? Do these passages support or undermine the theory of biblical inerrancy? Most Christians are more familiar with the New Testament than the Old Testament. Let me suggest, therefore, that we begin with the New Testament accounts of Judas Iscariot's fate.

1. Judas' Fate

In our gospels Judas, Jesus' betrayer, comes across as an ignoble person who met a tragic end. Both Matthew's gospel and the book of Acts contain accounts of Judas' sad fate. The account in Matthew 27:3-5 reads as follows:

> When Judas, his betrayer, saw that he was condemned, he repented and brought back the thirty pieces of silver to the chief priest and the elders, saying, "I have sinned in betraying innocent blood." They said, "What is that to us? See to it yourself." And throwing down the thirty pieces of silver in the temple, he departed; and he went and hanged himself.

This Matthean tradition teaches two things:

a. Judas took the thirty pieces of silver (the betrayal money) back to the temple priests.

b. Having thrown the silver coins down on the temple floor, Judas departed and committed suicide by hanging himself.

A contrary tradition concerning Judas' fate, however, appears in the book of Acts. The first chapter of Acts contains an account of the early church's decision to select a person to replace Judas. They chose Matthias as Judas' replacement (Acts 1:15-26). In the context of this episode there appears (Acts 1:18) a parenthetical remark about Judas' fate. This remark about Judas asserts,

> Now this man bought a field with the reward of his iniquity; and falling headlong he burst open in the middle and all his bowels gushed out.

This remark in Acts 1:18 teaches two things:

a. Judas took the betrayal money and purchased real estate—a field.

b. Judas died from a bizarre rupture of his body organs.

In both Matthew and Acts the field associated with Judas is called the "Field of Blood." In Acts 1:18 this field was purchased by Judas *before* his death; in Matthew 27:6-8, contrarily, this field was purchased by the temple priests *after* Judas' death.

Thus in Matthew 27 and Acts 1, four conflicting traditions concerning Judas' fate appear. Those four conflicting traditions are:

a. In Matthew's gospel Judas *returned the betrayal money to the temple priests*; in Acts, contrarily, Judas *purchased a field with the betrayal money.*

b. In Matthew's gospel Judas *committed suicide*; in Acts, contrarily, *he died from a puzzling illness* which involved a swelling and bursting of his body.

c. In Matthew's gospel the Field of Blood was purchased *by temple priests*; in Acts, contrarily, the Field of Blood was purchased *by Judas.*

d. In Matthew's gospel the Field of Blood was purchased *after* Judas' death; in Acts, contrarily, the Field of Blood was purchased *before* Judas' death.

Non-inerrantists contend these four diverse traditions contradict each other. To claim that all of them are true would violate Aristotle's Law of Non-contradiction.

2. Paul's Damascus Road Experience

The book of Acts contains three accounts (9:1-8; 22:4-16; 26:9-18) of Paul's Damascus Road experience. Instead of dealing with this episode in its entirety, I want us to concentrate on two details:

a. Did Paul's companions hear the heavenly voice?

b. Did Paul's companions stand, or did they fall to the ground?

Acts 9:7 reads as follows: "The men who were traveling with him *stood* speechless, *hearing the voice* but seeing no one." This verse relates that:

a. Paul's companions *stood*.

b. Paul's companions *heard* the heavenly voice.

Contrarily, however, the Damascus Road account in Acts 22:9 quotes Paul as saying, "Now those who were with me saw the light *but did not hear the voice of the one who was speaking to me.*" And in Acts 26:14 Paul observed that everyone who was with him fell to the ground. Thus a comparative reading of Acts 9:7, 22:9 and 26:14 reveals two contradictions:

a. Acts 9:7 states that Paul's companions *heard* the heavenly voice; contrarily, Acts 22:9 states they *did not hear* the heavenly voice.

b. Acts 9:7 states that Paul's companions *stood*; contrarily, Acts 26:14 states that they *fell to the ground*.

"Our comparative reading of Acts 9:7, 22:9, and 26:14 reveals opposing traditions about what happened to Paul's companions. We did not create these conflicting traditions. We simply have analyzed parallel biblical texts." So non-inerrantists reason. Having given attention to two New Testament episodes, I want us now to give attention to three Old Testament episodes.

3. The Time of the Divine Name's Revealing

Words like "Zeus" and "Asclepius" are reminders that in the ancient world the gods were given personal names. When speaking about cosmic powers the ancients did not use abstract expressions like "Ultimate Reality" or "ground of being." Rather, they used personal names like "Enlil" or "Shamash." Some Christians are unaware that the God of the Old Testament also has a personal name. This personal name is *Yahweh*. Spelled in Hebrew letters "Yahweh" looks like this: יהוה. In biblical studies these four Hebrew letters which constitute the divine name are referred to as the *Tetragrammaton*—a term which literally means "four letters." All Christians are familiar with words which are built upon the name Yahweh. For example, we have heard the word *hallelujah*, a term which appears time and again in the choruses of Handel's *Messiah*. *Hallelujah* means "praise Yahweh," and we are familiar with *Jesus*—a word which means "Yahweh saves."

A question which can be broached in biblical studies is: at what point in time (at what moment in history) did the Jews first learn that God's personal name was Yahweh? The book of Exodus suggests the Jews first learned about the name "Yahweh" during the time of Moses. This is implied in Exodus 6:2-3 which asserts,

> And God said to Moses, "I am Yahweh. I appeared to Abraham, to Isaac, and to Jacob as El Shaddai, but by my name of Yahweh I did not make myself known to them."

I ask you—the reader—to turn in your Bible to Exodus 6:2-3. Read these two verses. In all likelihood the name "Yahweh" does not appear. Nor (in all likelihood) does the phrase "El Shaddai." Instead, your translation probably reads something like this:

And God said to Moses, "I am the LORD. I appeared to Abraham, to Isaac, and to Jacob as God Almighty, but by my name the LORD I did not make myself known to them."

Such is the case because "God Almighty" is the literal meaning of the Hebrew words "El Shaddai." Moreover, you will notice in your Bible that "Yahweh" has been translated by "Lord" or "LORD." In the English-speaking world the custom has developed of using "Lord" to translate "Yahweh." In modern translations, like the Good News Bible or the Revised Standard Version, "Yahweh" is always rendered as "LORD" (all letters capitalized). By now you may be wondering: what does the word "Yahweh" mean? We don't know for a certainty what this name means. Dozens of meanings have been suggested. What we do know is that "Yahweh" (translated as "LORD") occurs hundreds of times in the Old Testament.

Returning to our main thought line, we are grappling with the issue of when the Jews learned God's personal name. Exodus 6:2-3, the passage quoted above, contains four assertions which bear on this issue.

a. Yahweh is God's personal name.

b. God disclosed his personal name (Yahweh) to Moses, the Exodus hero who lived in the thirteenth century before Christ. Exodus 3:14-15 also contains this disclosure-to-Moses tradition.

c. God disclosed himself as El Shaddai to Abraham, Isaac, and Jacob.

d. *But God did not not reveal his personal name Yahweh to Abraham, Isaac, and Jacob*—men who lived in the eighteenth century (hundreds of years before Moses).

I want us, bearing these four assertions in mind, to give attention now to the fifteenth chapter of Genesis. This chapter deals with Abraham—the Jewish patriarch who lived centuries prior to Moses. This chapter contains a report (contrary to the just-noted tradition in Exodus 6) *that God did disclose his personal name (Yahweh) to Abraham*. Indeed, Abraham used this personal name in prayer. Genesis 15:7-8 reads:

> And he (God) said to him, "I am the LORD (Yahweh) who brought you from Ur of the Chaldeans, to give you this land to possess." But he (Abraham) said, "O LORD (Yahweh) God, how am I to know that I shall possess it?"

Moreover, Genesis 28 contains a report (contrary to the Exodus 6 tradition noted above) *that God also revealed himself as Yahweh to Jacob*. Genesis 28:10-17 asserts:

> Jacob left Beersheba, and went toward Haran. And he came to a certain place, and stayed there that night, because the sun had set. Taking one of the stones of the place, he put it under his head and lay down in that place to sleep. And he dreamed that there was a ladder set up on the earth, and the top of it reached to heaven; and behold, the angels of God were ascending and descending on it! And behold, Yahweh stood above it and said, "I am Yahweh, the God of Abraham your father and the God of Isaac; the land on which you lie I will give to you and to your descendants; and your descendants shall be like the dust of the earth, and you shall spread abroad to the west and to the east and to the north and to the south; and by you and your descendants shall all the families of the earth bless themselves. Behold, I am with you and will keep you wherever you go, and will bring you back to this land; for I will not leave you until I have done that of which I have spoken to you." Then Jacob awoke from his sleep and said, "Surely Yahweh is in this place; and I did not know it."

And he was afraid, and said, "How awesome is this place! This is none other than the house of God, and this is the gate of heaven."

This just-quoted passage deals with Jacob's dream at Bethel. In this dream Yahweh appears to Jacob and says (Genesis 28:13), "I am Yahweh, the God of Abraham your father and the God of Isaac; the land on which you lie I will give to you and to your descendants." On awakening from the dream, Jacob affirmed (Genesis 28:16), "Surely Yahweh is in this place; and I did not know it."

Thus when we compare Genesis 15, Genesis 28, and Exodus 6, we encounter a dilemma. This dilemma can be stated as follows:

a. Exodus 6 asserts God did *not* reveal his personal name (Yahweh) to Abraham and to Jacob.

b. Yet Genesis 15 and 28 assert God *did* reveal his personal name (Yahweh) to Abraham and to Jacob.

Non-inerrantists reason: "You can't have it both ways. You can't simultaneously contend that God *did and did not* reveal his personal name–Yahweh–to Abraham and Jacob. To believe both of these assertions would be a logical incongruity." Thus—so non-inerrantists assert—a *contradiction* exists between the Yahweh-name-revealing tradition of Exodus 6 and the Yahweh-name-revealing tradition in Genesis 15 and Genesis 28. Non-inerrantists also assert: "We didn't create this Yahweh-name-revealing contradiction encountered in Genesis and Exodus. We have merely analyzed and compared various biblical texts." Parenthetically, the existence of such contradictions in the first five books of the Old Testament was one factor which led scholars in the nineteenth century to conclude that these books are a fusing of diverse sources which were originally independent and contained varying traditions.

Having given attention to the Yahweh-name-revealing conundrum, I want us now to turn to the King Jehoiachin puzzle.

4. Discrepancies Concerning King Jehoiachin

From approximately 1000 B.C. until Jerusalem's destruction by the Babylonians in 586 B.C. the Jews were ruled by kings. We read about the reigns of these kings in the Old Testament books of I and II Samuel, I and II Kings, and I and II Chronicles. Trying to understand this four-hundred-year monarchical period in Jewish history is—to put it mildly—perplexing. The characters (kings, prophets, priests and charlatans) and events are complex. Initially a series of kings (Saul, David, Solomon) ruled as sole monarchs over all the Jews. On King Solomon's death, however, a change occurred. Jews living in northern Palestine no longer wanted to be ruled by oppressive monarchs who resided in Jerusalem and loved to levy taxes. A revolt took place, and out of this revolt two minuscule Jewish states emerged. A petty state was founded in northern Palestine and became known as the Kingdom of Israel with its capital (eventually) at Samaria. A small state continued in southern Palestine; referred to as the Kingdom of Judah, its capital was Jerusalem. For decades these two Jewish states— each with its own line of kings—existed side by side. These kings, unfortunately for us, did not have easy-to-remember names like "King John" or "King Henry" or "King George." Instead, they had names like "Jehoash" and "Amaziah." The strangeness of the monarchs' names and the large number of these kings who ruled over these two petty Jewish states make this period of Jewish history difficult to comprehend. Moreover, two different accounts of the monarchical period appear in the Old Testament. One record of the era of Jewish kings appears in the books of Samuel and Kings. This account (I and II Samuel, I and II Kings) is a part of what Old Testament scholars refer to as the Deuteronomic history of the Jews. A second record of the era of Jewish kings is found in I and II Chronicles. Both of these accounts cover the same four-hundred-year period; they trace Jewish history from Saul, the first monarch, through Jerusalem's destruction in 586 B.C. by Babylon. Both records inform us of events which took place during the reigns of various Jewish kings. It is puzzling to note, however, that these parallel accounts (the one in I and II Samuel and I and II Kings and the one in I and II Chronicles) do not always agree. Between these two records discrepancies occur. I shall cite—for illustrative purposes—one or two of these discrepancies.

Take, for example, the reign of King Jehoiachin. Jehoiachin was one of the last monarchs of the kingdom of Judah which had Jerusalem as its capital. Jehoiachin's reign was a tragic time because the Jews were being threatened by the Babylonians under King Nebuchanezzar.

Parallel accounts of Jehoiachin's brief reign appear in II Kings 24 and II Chronicles 36. These accounts contain a discrepancy concerning *how old* Jehoiachin was when he *began* his reign as king in Jerusalem. II Kings 24:8 states, "Jehoiachin was *eighteen years old* when he became king, and he reigned *three months* in Jerusalem." Yet II Chronicles 36:9 states, "Jehoiachin was *eight years old* when he began to reign, and he reigned *three months and ten days* in Jerusalem." The first account informs us Jehoiachin was *eighteen* years old when he began to reign; the second account informs us he was *eight* years of age when he commenced his rule. Moreover, the first account asserts he reigned *three months* whereas the second account states he ruled *three months and ten days*. Both accounts agree Jehoiachin was deported to Babylon and was succeeded by King Zedekiah (II Kings 24:14-17, II Chronicles 36:10). These parallel accounts, however, do not agree on Zedekiah's identity. The first account identifies Zedekiah as Jehoiachin's *uncle* (II Kings 24:17) while the second account identifies Zedekiah as Jehoiachin's *brother* (II Chronicles 36:10).

Questions emerge. Was Jehoiachin *eight* or *eighteen years* of age when he became king in Jerusalem? Did he rule for *three months* or for *three months and ten days*? Was Zedekiah an *uncle* or a *brother* of Jehoiachin? Assuming Jehoiachin was an eight-year-old king who ruled for three months, how was he able to become a polygamist whose wives were deported with him to Babylon (II Kings 24:15)? The parallel Jehoiachin accounts in II Kings and II Chronicles contain at least three discrepancies:

a. A discrepancy appears concerning Jehoiachin's age when he became king in Jerusalem. One account states he was *eight* years old. Another account states he was *eighteen* years old. This age difference is similar to the discrepancy concerning King Ahaziah's age when he began to rule. II Kings 8:26 states that Ahaziah, king of Judah, was *twenty-two years old* when he began to reign. Yet II Chronicles 22:2 states that Ahaziah was *forty-two years old* when he began his rule.

b. A discrepancy appears concerning the length of Jehoiachin's reign. One account states he ruled for *three months*; another account states he ruled for *three months and ten days*.

c. A discrepancy appears concerning the relationship between Jehoiachin and Zedekiah. One account states Zedekiah was Jehoiachin's *uncle*. Another account states Zedekiah was Jehoiachin's *brother*.

Again, non-inerrantists observe, "We didn't create these discrepancies concerning Jehoiachin's coronation age, reign length, and successor. All we have done is to analyze and compare different biblical texts." I want us to turn now to the puzzle concerning the molten sea of Solomon's temple.

5. The Capacity and Circumference of Solomon's Molten Sea

Every reader of the Bible has heard about Solomon's temple, a house of worship built by King Solomon in Jerusalem. An account of the building of Solomon's temple appears in I Kings, chapters 6-8. A second account of the temple's construction appears in II Chronicles, chapters 3-7. These accounts tell us about artisans who worked on the temple and about materials used in its construction. We are informed about the temple's decorations and furnishings. Among the furnishings was a molten sea (described in I Kings 7:23-26 and II Chronicles 4:1-6), a vessel which priests used for washing. When we say this vessel was molten, we mean it was made by melting and casting metal. Cast by Hiram of Tyre, the molten sea was made of bronze which David had taken as spoil (I Chronicles 18:8). It was a complex artistic work. Decorated with gourds, the molten sea consisted of a basin which rested upon twelve bronze oxen, facing at right angles in four directions. Its thickness was a handbreath, and its brim was turned outward, giving the appearance of a cup, "like the flower of a lily."

The accounts in I Kings and II Chronicles agree the molten sea was five cubits high (the estimated length of a Hebrew cubit is 17.5 inches). Both accounts agree it was circular in shape ("ten cubits from brim to brim" and "a line of thirty cubits measured its circumference"). Yet a discrepancy occurs concerning the amount of water the molten sea could hold. I Kings 7:26 states its capacity was *two thousand baths* (a *bath* is a Hebrew unit of liquid measure estimated to be 22 liters). Reflecting a variant tradition, II Chronicles 4:5 states its capacity was *over three thousand baths*. Which volume is correct? *Two thousand baths* or *three thousand baths*? Or to use contemporary measures, *ten thousand gallons* or *fifteen thousand gallons*? Non-inerrantists are not certain.

Moreover, both accounts (I Kings 7:23, II Chronicles 4:2) state that the ratio of the circular sea's diameter to circumference was one to three ("ten cubits from brim to brim" and "a line of thirty cubits measured its circumference"). This ratio produces the curious formula $C=3d$ (circumference equals the diameter multiplied by three). But this formula is a geometric impossibility. The correct formula for a circle's circumference is $C=\pi d$. The Old Testament's description of Solomon's molten sea involves a geometric impossibility.

Thus—by way of recapitulation—from the five issues just analyzed (the time of the revealing of Yahweh's name, Jehoiachin's coronation age, Solomon's molten sea, Judas' fate and Paul's Damascus Road experience) the following conundrums have emerged:

1. The Bible teaches Yahweh's name was *not known* prior to Moses; contrarily, it teaches Yahweh's name *was known* prior to Moses. Indeed, Genesis 4:1 teaches Yahweh's name was known to Eve, Adam's wife.

2. The Bible affirms Yahweh's name *was not* known to Abraham; contrarily, it affirms Yahweh's name *was* known to Abraham.

3. The Bible contends Yahweh's name was *unknown* to Jacob; contrarily, it contends Yahweh's name *was known* to Jacob.

4. The Bible states Jehoiachin was *eighteen* years old when he began to reign; contrarily, it states Jehoiachin was *eight* years old when he began to rule.

5. The Bible asserts Jehoiachin ruled for *three months*; contrarily, it asserts Jehoiachin ruled for *three months and ten days*.

6. The Bible suggests Zedekiah was Jehoiachin's *uncle*; contrarily, it suggests Zedekiah was Jehoiachin's *brother*.

7. The Bible notes Ahaziah was *twenty-two years old* when he began to rule; contrarily, it notes Ahaziah was *forty-two years* old when he began to reign.

8. The Bible presents a geometric impossibility: a circle with a circumference equaling its diameter multiplied by three.

9. The Bible describes the molten sea in Solomon's temple as having a capacity of *two thousand* baths; contrarily, it describes the same molten sea as having a capacity of over *three thousand* baths.

10. The Bible records that Judas *returned the betrayal money to the temple*; contrarily, it records he *purchased real estate* (a field) with the betrayal money.

11. The Bible says Judas *committed suicide* by hanging himself; contrarily, it says Judas *died from a rupture of body organs.*

12. The Bible declares the Field of Blood was purchased by *Judas during his lifetime;* contrarily, it declares the Field of Blood was purchased by the *temple priests after Judas' death.*

13. The Bible relates that Paul's companions on the Damascus Road *heard* the heavenly voice; contrarily, it relates they *did not hear* the heavenly voice.

14. The Bible states that Paul's companions on the Damascus Road *stood*; contrarily, it relates that they *fell to the ground.*

These fourteen conundrums, arbitrarily chosen because of their specificity and obviousness, are well-known in biblical studies. Commentaries and biblical encyclopedias regularly take note of them. They are illustrative of minor contradictions, errors, and slip-ups which occur in Holy Scripture. The existence of these minor conundrums makes it impossible for non-inerrantists to accept the claim that the Bible is inerrant.

But these minor puzzles (puzzles like Judas' fate or Jehoiachin's correct coronation age) do not fully illuminate the disagreement between inerrantists and non-inerrantists. Their disagreement has a deeper dimension.

Non-inerrantists hold that the Bible contains viewpoints which no clear-thinking person in our time accepts. They do not hesitate to label some biblical attitudes as untenable because they are "time-conditioned." In other words, the biblical authors lived within culturally-determined conceptual horizons which make some of their beliefs obsolete.

Take, for example, the biblical attitude toward *human slavery*. No sensitive person in our day believes that one person has a legal or moral right to own (as property) a fellow human being. All of us deem slavery, an inhumane relationship, to be morally repulsive. Yet the Bible takes human slavery for granted. This fact is disguised in our English translations by such euphemisms as "man-servant" and "maid-servant." Nowhere in biblical literature is slavery explicitly condemned. Instead, the Bible contains passages like Leviticus 25:44-46 which asserts:

> As for your male and female slaves whom you may have: you may buy male and female slaves from among the nations that are round you. You may also buy from among the strangers who sojourn with you and their families that are with you, who have been born on your land; and they may be your property. You may bequeath them to your sons after you, to inherit as a possession forever.

In Exodus 21:20-21 a slave is recognized as being his master's property. This passage reads:

> If a man takes a stick and beats his slave, whether male or female, and the slave dies on the spot, the man is to be punished. But if the slave does not die for a day or two, the master is not to be punished. The loss of his property is punishment enough.

The law of Moses contains detailed slave legislation dealing with such matters as drilling a hole through a slave's ear (Exodus 21:6), selling a daughter into slavery (Exodus 21:7), and knocking out a slave's eye or tooth (Exodus 21:26-27). Ephesians spells out guidelines for proper slave behavior (Ephesians 6:5-8). The letter to Philemon concerns Onesimus, a runaway slave sent back to his owner by St. Paul. Indeed, the Bible carries the institution of slavery all the way back to Noah (Genesis 9:25-27).

Thus we confront the insight: on the issue of human slavery the Bible is a product ("a child") of the era wherein it was written. It is historically conditioned. Slavery was an entrenched institution in the ancient Middle East and in the Roman empire. The Old Testament, written against a Middle Eastern background, and the New Testament, composed in the context of the Roman empire, presuppose human slavery. The biblical acceptance of slavery, an obnoxious institution, is an example of *cultural relativism*—the sociological theory that what we believe on various issues is at times molded by the cultural-historical setting in which we live. Our views are "time-conditioned." No person lives thousands of years ahead of his era. The inescapability of cultural relativism has a bearing on the inerrancy controversy. Non-inerrantists candidly admit that the Bible's slavery acceptance is unfortunate. This slave legislation makes it impossible for them to claim it is inerrant in *all* its teachings. Indeed, to claim that Holy Scripture is inerrant in its slavery support would be ethical suicide.

Human slavery, however, is merely one example of the Bible's entrapment by cultural relativism. Consider, for example, its "time-conditioned" view of the *earth's age* and *shape*. A commonplace in science is the view that our earth has existed for a long time period. Indeed, geologists, basing their views on a study of fossils and rock formations, contend the earth is billions of years old. This concept of earth's antiquity, however, was unknown in the ancient world and was unknown to biblical writers. A study of the Bible's time system reveals that its authors believed the earth was created around 4000 B.C., giving it a lifespan from its beginning until the present of approximately 6,000 years (incomplete evidence supporting this statement I am relegating to an endnote).[1]

The view that the earth is only several thousand years old prevailed in early Christian thought. St. Augustine, a Christian thinker who lived in the fifth century during the Roman empire's collapse, expressed the view that less than 6,000 years had elapsed from the world's creation to his own day. This view prevailed into the seventeenth century when Archbishop James Usher, taking at face value the chronological statements in Genesis, calculated that the earth was created in 4004 B.C. Usher's view was further refined by another English divine who concluded the earth was created at nine o'clock in the morning on October 23. Bibles are still printed inserting in the margin beside Genesis 1:1 ("In the beginning God created the heavens and the earth") the date—4004 B.C.—calculated by Usher. The Bible *does* support the view that the earth came into existence around 4000 B.C. Non-inerrantists, accepting geological evidence concerning earth's antiquity, conclude the Bible—as far as its chronology is concerned—is wrong. Moreover, they refuse to engage in specious reasoning to avoid this conclusion.

Likewise, non-inerrantists find it impossible to accept the Bible's view of the earth's shape (cosmology). Every schoolboy knows the earth resembles a ball. The earth's spherical shape, however, was unknown in the ancient world and did not become common coin in the realm of ideas until the fifteenth and sixteenth centuries after the global explorations of Columbus, Drake, and Magellan. Unaware of earth's sphericity, our forefathers—following "common sense"—believed the world was flat. Biblical writers, children of their time, shared this view of the earth being a horizontal plane with edges and corners.[2]

Moreover, throughout the Bible there is the presupposition of the universe being like a storied house with three floors: heaven, earth, and the netherworld. Heaven was the "top floor" (up in the sky) and was God's dwelling place or throne (Isaiah 66:1). Heaven was close to earth. This closeness explains why Jacob could dream of a ladder reaching from the earth to heaven (Genesis 28:12). At Jesus' baptism heaven was opened, and a divine voice, audible on earth, spoke to him (Mark 1:9-11). Toward the close of his defense before the Jerusalem mob, Stephen looked up into heaven and saw God's glory and Jesus standing on the right side of God (Acts 7:55).

Whereas heaven was "above" this earth, the netherworld—the realm of the dead—was located "below." In the Old Testament this netherworld is called *Sheol.* On occasion the earth physically opened and allowed people to fall headlong into the netherworld. This happened, for example, to Korah, Dathan, Abiram and their families. Thus Numbers 16:31-34 recounts:

> As soon as Moses had finished speaking, the ground under Dathan and Abiram split open and swallowed them and their families, together with all of Korah's followers and their possessions. So they went down alive to the world of the dead (*Sheol*) with their possessions. The earth closed over them and they vanished. All the people of Israel who were there fled when they heard their cry. They shouted, "Run! The earth might swallow us too!"

Non-inerrantists have no qualms about asserting that biblical cosmology (the conception of the cosmos as a three-storied house) is the cosmology of the ancient Near East and is unbelievable to modern man.

A final example which I shall cite of biblical materials non-inerrantists do not accept at face value is the *variety of God concepts* encountered in the Bible. In early stages of the biblical tradition God is conceived in anthropomorphic terms. By this I mean God is conceived as a "big man." He has a body, walks with Adam in the cool of the evening, appears to Moses on Mt. Sinai, and visits with the elders of Israel. However, in later stages of the biblical tradition God is conceived as an incorporeal spirit, without limitations of a body. As a potent spirit he is able to will things into existence, to create merely by a fiat such as "let there be light." Concerning this invisible God the Fourth Gospel asserts, "No man has ever seen God." Thus in one part of the Bible men "see" God and walk and talk with him; yet in another part of the Bible God is conceived as an invisible spirit whom no man can "see." Inquisitive religionists contend these concepts are contradictory; it is impossible to believe both in a "big man" God who strolls in the Garden of Eden while conversing with Adam and in a "spiritual" God who is invisible.

The illustrations could go on and on of biblical episodes, viewpoints, and assertions which non-inerrantists deem to be problematic and which preclude for them an assumption of biblical inerrancy. Indeed, they contend that a commitment to inerrancy *raises more problems than it solves* (problems which inerrantists either ignore or of which they are unaware).

Our primary task has not been to decide whether non-inerrantists are right or wrong. Instead, our task has been to understand why they reason as they do. Maybe their understanding of biblical inerrantism is inaccurate. Or maybe they are wrong in broaching the questions they raise. But if they are in fact a mistaken group, then inerrantists have a Christian responsibility to help them understand the error of their ways. It is not enough for inerrantists to throw verbal stones at non-inerrantists by saying, "You're dishonoring the Bible in suggesting it contains puzzling, problematic passages!" Inerrantist spokesmen need to explain why biblical materials which non-inerrantists judge to be conundrums are in fact *not* conundrums. Moreover, they should present their explanations in writing. I emphasize the words *in writing*. A written explanation permits reflection and public scrutiny.

I will illustrate what I mean by appealing to the Jehoiachin coronation-age puzzle which was discussed earlier in this chapter. About this puzzle non-inerrantists reason as follows: "At one point the Bible states Jehoiachin was eight years old when he became king in Jerusalem. At another place—curiously—it states he was eighteen years old when he became king. Thus we encounter a dilemma. Was Jehoiachin eight or eighteen years of age when he became a Jewish ruler? We could 'solve' this dilemma by holding that one of these coronation ages (either eight or eighteen) is right while the other one is wrong. But what we cannot hold (as inerrantism requires) is: the Bible is correct in asserting Jehoiachin was *eight* years old when he became king, *and* the Bible is correct in asserting he was *eighteen* years old when he became king. This would be a logical incongruity, a violation of the logician's truth table. Thus we reluctantly conclude that the Bible contains contradictory traditions concerning Jehoiachin's coronation age." So non-inerrantists reason. For the sake of our discussion let us assume they are *wrong* in their reasoning concerning Jehoiachin. Let us assume the two coronation-age traditions are reconcilable (an assumption demanded by inerrantism). Inerrantists, I suggest, have an obligation to explain in writing how Jehoiachin was both eight and eighteen years old when he became king of the Jews. I emphasize again the words *in writing* for a written explanation permits public examination. Non-inerrantists, I suggest, would find it illuminating to peruse an inerrantist explanation of how Jehoiachin was *simultaneously eight and eighteen years old* when he became king in Jerusalem. Yet, to my knowledge, inerrantists have not provided such a written explanation, and this failure is unfortunate. Inerrantists commendably excel in oratory. But the primary object of oratory is persuasion; its primary object is not seeking the truth. Inerrantists should lower the tone of their oratory and invest more energy in careful exegesis and reasoned discourse in order to provide non-inerrantists with written answers to the questions they broach.

❦

NOTES

[1]Any inquisitive person can gain insight into the Bible's time system by looking at the "genealogy" in Luke 3:23-38. This genealogy purports to carry Jesus' family lineage back to Adam. In Jewish thought Adam was the first man fashioned by God at the time of the world's creation (Genesis 1-3). A perusal of this genealogy reveals seventy-seven generations from Adam to Jesus. Allowing the round number of fifty years for each generation, this genealogy suggests there were approximately 3,850 years from Adam to Jesus. Taken at face value, Luke's genealogy shows no awareness of the age of the human race as revealed by anthropological research. No anthropologist would defend the view that the human race came into existence a scant 3,850 years prior to the birth of Jesus.

Any inquisitive person can also gain insight into biblical chronology by reading Genesis 5, 7:11, 9:28, and 11:10-32. A reading of these passages (for an analysis of these data see the article "Chronology of the Old Testament," by S. J. De Vries , on pp. 580-599 of Vol. I of *The Interpreter's Dictionary of the Bible*, published by Abingdon Press, Nashville) reveals that in Old Testament thought approximately 1,950 years elapsed from the creation of the world until Abraham who lived in the second millenium before the beginning of the Christian era. These calculations place the creation of the world around 4000 B. C. Thus the Old Testament shows no awareness of earth's antiquity as suggested by geological research.

Yet the Bible's time system was accepted by the Church. Thus Lactantius, a church father who lived A. D. 260-330, believed the earth was less than 6,000 years old; moreover, he believed that when the earth became 6,000 years old "the end of time" would arrive. In *The Divine Institutes* he wrote:

> Plato and many others of the philosophers, since they were ignorant of the origins of all things, and of that primal period at which the world was made, said that many thousands of years had passed since this beautiful arrangement of the world was completed. But we, whom the Holy Scriptures instruct to the knowledge of the truth, know the beginning and the end of the world. Therefore let the philosophers, who enumerate thousands of ages from the beginning of the world, know that the six thousandth year is not yet completed. Therefore, since all the works of God were completed in six days, the world must continue in its present state six ages, that is, six thousand years.

An account of the struggle between science and religion over geological and anthropological evidence can be found in chapters v and vi of Andrew White, *A History of the Warfare of Science with Theology* (New York: George Braziller, 1955).

[2]Numerous books and articles discuss the correlations between Near Eastern thought and biblical thought concerning the shape of the earth. Available in most libraries is the article by T. H. Gaster on "Earth" in Vol. II of *The Interpreter's Dictionary of the Bible* (Nashville: Abingdon Press, 1962). Biblical writers conceived of the earth as being square in shape. "After this I saw four angels standing at the four corners of the earth, holding back the four winds of the earth, that no wind might blow on earth or sea or against any tree" (Revelation 7:1). A similar idea is expressed in Isaiah 11:12 and Ezekiel 7:2.

CHAPTER THREE

❦

A Conversation among an Inerrantist, a Non-Inerrantist, and a Bystander

BYSTANDER:

As all three of us know, several denominations today are having Donnybrooks over how the Bible is to be read and understood. Some go so far as to call these intra-denominational conflicts "holy wars." Let me ask you, an inerrantist, to spell out for us what you think the root issue is in this controversy.

INERRANTIST:

The root issue, as I see it, concerns the attitude Christians should have toward Holy Scripture. Is the Bible God-inspired? Is it *completely* true and void of errors? Or—as non-inerrantists believe—is it a document with mistakes and a book containing viewpoints we can no longer accept? We've got two possibilities: the Bible is either fallible or infallible. There's no doubt in my mind which of these alternatives is right. To me the Bible is infallible; it's true from the first verse of Genesis to the last one in the Revelation of John. This is what most Christians believe today. It's what most have believed in the past, and I contend we ought to hold to what *is* and *has been* the *dominant view* in the church about the Bible.

NON-INERRANTIST:

I've heard this opinion expressed before. "We ought to believe what the majority believes." Philosophers have an expression for this way of reasoning; they refer to it as the *argumentum ad populum*, a Latin phrase which means "an argument from the multitude." "Believe as the masses do. What the majority accepts is true." There are times when this argument holds, and I have no difficulty accepting the view that time and again the masses are right. But are they *always* right? Does it follow that in *every* situation we should accept what the majority believes? For centuries most people believed the earth was flat, and they believed the sun revolved around it. But astronomers like Copernicus and Galileo (anticipated by Aristarchus and Eratosthenes) came along and taught the earth moves and revolves around the sun. We now know they were right. Yet in their day people said about Copernicus and Galileo: "They're crazy!" In this instance the unpopular minority was right while the convinced majority was wrong. Similarly, it may be that many Christians in the past believed in biblical inerrancy. And it may be that many are inerrantists today. But the mere fact that a large number hold to inerrancy doesn't make this viewpoint true.

INERRANTIST:

I still say you can't ignore what the masses believe.

NON-INERRANTIST:

I'm not suggesting you can or should ignore what the masses believe. All I'm contending is: you don't decide what's true by counting noses and then letting a majority vote dominate. Counting noses to determine truth is a dubious procedure.

INERRANTIST:

The reason the majority believes the Bible is infallible is because that's the claim the Bible makes for itself. We inerrantists take our stand on II Timothy 3:16. "All scripture is given by inspiration of God, and is profitable for doctrine, for reproof, for correction, for instruction in righteousness." There you have it—the inerrantist view of scripture in a *nutshell*. The Bible itself claims to be infallibly inspired.

NON-INERRANTIST:

You're right in saying II Timothy 3:16 is the proof-text *par excellence* of inerrantism. Inerrantists like James I. Packer are constantly quoting it. Would you repeat II Timothy 3:16 for me? I'm not sure I heard it correctly.

INERRANTIST:

I'll be glad to repeat it. "All scripture is given by inspiration of God, and is profitable for doctrine, for reproof, for correction, for instruction in righteousness."

NON-INERRANTIST:

You contend this verse "proves" the Bible is *infallible*. Or to use the other word you like to use—*inerrant*. I didn't hear either "inerrant" or "infallible" when you quoted II Timothy 3:16.

INERRANTIST:

It may be that the words "inerrant" and "infallible" don't actually appear. But they're implied. That's what we inerrantists believe "inspired" entails. Being inspired means that every word, every fact, every idea found in the Bible is true. Otherwise, it wouldn't be inspired. *Inspiration guarantees inerrancy.*

NON-INERRANTIST:

"All scripture is inspired." What do you think the word "scripture" in this statement refers to?

INERRANTIST:

All the books in the Bible. The thirty-nine in the Old Testament and the twenty-seven in the New Testament. Add them together and you've got sixty-six. "All scripture" in II Timothy 3:16 refers to the sixty-six books that compose the Bible.

NON-INERRANTIST:

Are you sure?

INERRANTIST:

Yes, I'm sure. Aren't you?

NON-INERRANTIST:

No, I'm not.

INERRANTIST:

Why?

NON-INERRANTIST:

I'm not certain because a study of the Bible's historical development shows that II Timothy 3:16 is asserting something quite different. When II Timothy 3:16 was written back in the first century, the New Testament as we know it today hadn't come into existence. The New Testament as we have it didn't shape up until the fourth century of the Christian era. The earliest document which lists the twenty-seven books of the New Testament as they appear in today's Bibles is a fourth-century letter composed by Bishop Athanasius of Alexandria. That's some three hundred years after II Timothy 3:16 was written; there's no way under the shining sun that this verse can refer to our New Testament. In the first century—when II Timothy 3:16 was written—our twenty-seven document New Testament didn't even exist. Nor can this verse refer to the thirty-nine-document Old Testament which we read today. Earlier Old Testaments contained books which were later removed from the Bible. I'm referring to the books of the Apocrypha—works like *Tobit* and *Ecclesiasticus.* Martin Luther, sixteenth-century reformer, removed these Apocrypha books—some fifteen in number—from the Old Testament and put them in a separate collection between the Old Testament and the New Testament. Then the Puritans came along later and removed them from the Bible completely. To be on the level: the church has never universally agreed on which collection of books constitutes the Bible.

INERRANTIST:

Hold it a moment. If I understood you correctly, you just said, "The church has never universally agreed on which collection of books constitutes the Bible." I don't believe that statement is correct.

NON-INERRANTIST:

To the contrary, it is correct. For centuries the church's Bible was the Latin Vulgate. The Vulgate contained the fifteen books of the Apocrypha plus the books of the Old and New Testaments with which we are familiar. In 1546, the Council of Trent decreed that the canon of the Old Testament included the books of the Apocrypha (except the *Prayer of Manasseh* and I and II *Esdras*) and condemned anyone who did not accept them as sacred. Contrariwise, the Puritans, settlers of New England, decided to take the Apocryphal books out of the Old Testament because originally they had been written in Greek rather than Hebrew. Many pulpit Bibles, curiously, have the Apocryphal books but seldom—if ever—are they read in church services. More-over, some of our earliest and most-valued biblical manuscripts—like the famous *Codex Sinaiticus*—contain works such as the *Shepherd of Hermas* and the *Letter of Barnabas* which are not included in today's Bibles. So what's the conclusion? The Bible of Roman Catholicism is not identical with the Bible of grassroots Protestantism. Protestantism's Bible today is not identical with Protestantism's Bible back in the sixteenth century. Pulpit Bibles are not identical with most Bibles owned by people sitting on pews. When inerrantists declare that the Bible is inerrant, which Bible are they referring to? They are being arbitrary if they contend that "scripture" in II Timothy 3:16 refers to a Protestant Bible of sixty-six books. And on top of this, II Timothy 3:16 doesn't say what inerrantists think it says.

INERRANTIST:

What do you mean?

NON-INERRANTIST:

The text of II Timothy 3:16 doesn't say all scripture. Instead, the Greek text literally reads "*every* scripture." It's singular, not plural. The verse emphasizes the distributive, not the collective idea. A word-for-word translation is: "Every inspired writing (is) profitable for doctrine, for reproof, for correction, for instruction in righteousness." There's no way this *singular* assertion can apply to *all* the sixty-six documents of the typical Protestant Bible. That won't wash.

INERRANTIST:

I'm certain I could find a hundred scholars who could defend the way inerrantists interpret II Timothy 3:16. But let's don't get bogged down in a squabble over Greek words. Instead, let's get back to the main issue we're discussing—biblical infallibility. You don't understand how critical inerrancy is for Christianity. To be effective the Christian faith must have a standard for its beliefs. We need a source of authority. And that's what the Bible is for those of us who are inerrantists. We're not wishy-washy like you are. *If the Bible says it, we believe it.* It's that simple. We believe *all* the Bible. You want to be selective. You want to pick and choose. We feel that's arrogant, and we believe it's a dangerous procedure.

NON-INERRANTIST:

Did Jesus accept *all* the Bible?

INERRANTIST:

Of course he did.

NON-INERRANTIST:

I don't agree with you. He didn't accept the Old Testament's divorce law. The Law of Moses provided for divorce, but Jesus taught that this divorce provision was given because of mankind's hardness of heart and ought to be rejected. Moreover, he didn't accept the Old Testament's food laws. And the early church didn't accept the Old

Testament's teaching on circumcision. That's what vexes me about you inerrantists. You want to require Christians to adopt today a theological position which both Jesus and the early church rejected. And it's a theological position you inerrantists reject in practice. There's a gap as wide as the Grand Canyon between your theory and your practice.

INERRANTIST:

I challenge that statement as being untrue. You can't cite one verse in the Bible which we inerrantists don't believe and practice. Believing and practicing all the Bible—that's what makes us inerrantists.

NON-INERRANTIST:

You don't demand circumcision of converts—a demand which both the Old Testament and the conservative wing of the early church required. You don't accept Paul's demand that women be silent in church. Show me one church where women are silent. They sing, play musical instruments, and teach Bible classes. Women keep many churches going. In fact, one feature of the contemporary church is its effeminization. You inerrantists don't live by the Bible's food laws. You eat catfish, oysters, shrimp, and lobsters—all prohibited by Mosaic law. How long has it been since you got outraged over eating bacon or sausage for breakfast or oysters on the half-shell? Yet the Bible prohibits all of these foods. That's why orthodox Jews refuse to eat pork or shellfish.

INERRANTIST:

In expounding on pork and shellfish you're going down a side alley. Let's get back to the major issue. You can't get away from the insight that a Christian majority has always believed in biblical inerrancy. That's the ball we ought to keep our eyes on—not sausage and lobsters.

NON-INERRANTIST:

You keep pounding on the idea that a Christian majority has always believed in inerrancy. To hear you talk you'd think a belief in inerrancy goes all the way back to the first century. How long do you think the inerrancy theory has been around? *Inerrancy* doesn't appear in the church's vocabulary until the turn of this century—less than a hundred years ago. The inerrancy premise is a Johnny-come-lately on the scene of Christian beliefs. It was conceived by evangelicals who lived in the North—many of them Presbyterians—who were perplexed by the historical-critical method of biblical studies. Thinking they could settle controversial issues by passing resolutions, they voted inerrancy into the church's belief-system in hostile reaction to the emerging historical-critical method which they feared. They feared the historical-critical method because they didn't understand it.

INERRANTIST:

You've just broached a relevant issue, and one which I feel strongly about—the historical-critical method. This method is a pain and an embarrassment. It really is. And where within the church is this method thriving? You know the answer as well as I do. Within institutions of higher learning—particularly within seminaries. We're sending our young people to seminaries to study for the clergy, and our seminaries are destroying their faith by exposing them to the historical-critical method.

NON-INERRANTIST:

You've made an incredibly puzzling remark. You've said seminarians are having their faith destroyed by being exposed to the historical-critical method. *Can a destructible faith be authentic faith?* If a person's faith can be demolished, is it valid? Maybe the demolishing of destructible faith is a blessing in disguise. Or maybe the "faith" being destroyed is not authentic but counterfeit faith—a spurious understanding of the Christian religion. So let's be candid: many students enter our seminaries bloated with simplistic ideas which need to be destroyed.

INERRANTIST:

Simplistic ideas? Such as?

NON-INERRANTIST:

Such as your simplistic belief that the Bible contains no errors, no contradictions, no problematic statements. Any person who reads the Bible with open eyes and an open mind cannot avoid encountering puzzling statements. In one place the Bible tells us Judas returned his betrayal money to the Jewish priests; in another place it informs us he purchased a field with the betrayal money. That's a discrepancy. In one place the Bible tells us David bought a threshing floor for fifty shekels of silver; in another place it informs us he bought the same threshing floor for six hundred shekels of gold. That's another discrepancy. I can cite scores of biblical statements which belie the inerrancy theory. That's why non-inerrantists find it impossible to be inerrantists. We take seriously the phenomena of the text. We carefully analyze biblical passages. We let the Bible affirm what it affirms. You inerrantists either ignore the phenomena of the text or you transform yourselves into mental pretzels in attempting to explain away or to harmonize problematic passages.

INERRANTIST:

What you've just said reveals that you don't understand inerrantism. Maybe the biblical texts we have today contain puzzles. This I'll concede momentarily for the sake of argument. But when we inerrantists contend the biblical texts have no mistakes, we're referring to the texts as they were originally written. Inerrancy, we believe, characterized the autographs—the biblical books as originally composed.

NON-INERRANTIST:

You mean, for example, the first manuscript of Matthew or the first copy of Genesis?

INERRANTIST:

Right. Inerrantism applies to these works as they came from their authors' hands.

NON-INERRANTIST:

I see. Where would I go to look at the autograph—the original copy—of Matthew or Genesis? Would I go to the Vatican library in Rome or to the Church of the Holy Sepulcher in Jerusalem or to the Monastery of St. Catherine on the Sinai Peninsula? Where are the autographs of the Bible's sixty-six books located?

INERRANTIST:

They've all perished. None exists.

NON-INERRANTIST:

Am I understanding you to say we don't have the original copy of a single book in the Bible?

INERRANTIST:

That's right. They've all been lost or destroyed.

NON-INERRANTIST:

Then I find myself perplexed. Since the autographs no longer exist and since you have never seen them, how can you be certain they were inerrant? How can you describe or dogmatize over documents you've never seen or read? I suggest that believing that no-longer-existing autographs were inerrant is comparable to believing in the pot of gold at the end of the rainbow. Of what use to us is this pot of gold if we can never find it? Similarly, of what use are inerrant autographs if we can never have access to them? I perceive that inerrantists actually subscribe to a conjectured or speculative inerrancy. You're guilty of leaping into the dark.

INERRANTIST:

We're not jumping into the dark; instead, we're taking a leap of faith. By faith we believe the original biblical manuscripts were infallible. Maybe errors did creep into them as they were copied and then recopied across the centuries. But we believe the autographs were error-free. God guaranteed their inerrancy.

NON-INERRANTIST:

If God guaranteed that the autographs were inerrant, why did he not also guarantee across the centuries the transmission of error-free copies? Particularly if—as you contend—an error-free biblical text is of crucial importance for the Christian faith? But let's move on to another matter. I contend the typical inerrantist has never pondered the dilemma inerrantism encounters when it comes to language. And by language I'm referring primarily to words used in the Bible.

INERRANTIST:

I'm glad you've raised that issue. That's a dimension of inerrantism which many people don't understand. When it comes to language, we inerrantists don't waffle. We believe the *very words* used in the Bible are inspired. Every term in biblical literature has been divinely chosen.

NON-INERRANTIST:

Are you referring to the terms used in the original manuscripts of biblical books?

INERRANTIST:

You're on target. When we talk about every word being inspired, we're referring to words which appear in the autographs.

NON-INERRANTIST:

Do all inerrantists have a mastery of Hebrew, Aramaic, and Greek?

INERRANTIST:

Why do you ask that? What have Hebrew, Aramaic, and Greek to do with inerrantism?

NON-INERRANTIST:

They have a lot to do with inerrantism. Hebrew, Aramaic, and Greek are the languages in which the autographs were written. The biblical words inspired by God were—on the inerrancy theory—from these three languages. Thus the only people who have access to these inspired words—hence to an inerrant Bible—are people with a fluent, detailed knowledge of Hebrew, Aramaic, and Greek.

INERRANTIST:

That's a ridiculous idea.

NON-INERRANTIST:

It's not a ridiculous idea. A particular language's syntax, its words, and the meanings and connotations people associate with those words are all intertwined and are distinctive to that language. The translating of a written text from one language to another is always partial and approximate. That's why a person who reads the Bible only in translation—whether English or Spanish or German—could never be a practicing inerrantist. And I think you'll agree with me when I suggest that acquiring a fluent, detailed knowledge of Hebrew, Aramaic, and Greek is a demanding intellectual requirement. Particularly when you bear in mind that two of them—Hebrew and Aramaic—are Semitic rather than Indo-European languages. Most lay persons have no knowledge of them. Nor does the typical clergyman. In fact, most seminaries no longer require seminarians to study Hebrew, Aramaic, and Greek.

INERRANTIST:

I think what you're saying is unjustified. You're trying to make inerrantism hopelessly complicated. I believe I can be an inerrantist while reading a King James Bible. Or any other English translation.

NON-INERRANTIST:

Impossible, utterly impossible. Inerrantism cannot apply to the very words used in today's English Bibles because the English language—as we know it—wasn't in existence when the Bible was written. And as I've just observed, no two English translations are alike, and all of them render the original texts approximately, not completely. But even if you learned Hebrew like a Jerusalem Jew and Greek like an Athenian, you're still up against what I think is an insurmountable problem for inerrantism.

INERRANTIST:

What problem?

NON-INERRANTIST:

The problem of hermeneutics. Of interpretation. This problem is rooted in language's symbolic nature. Words, as every linguist knows, are symbols. Words in and of themselves—whether written or spoken—possess no meaning. They must be recognized and interpreted by the human mind which in turn invests words with meaning. Word meanings exist in the mental world, not in words *per se*. Thus inerrancy requires *infallible interpreters* who with certainty know word meanings and who know how to interpret biblical texts inerrantly. All of this blows my mind. The inerrancy theory demands inerrant Hebrew, Aramaic, and Greek texts (which inerrantists admit do not exist) plus language specialists who have detailed knowledge of Hebrew, Aramaic, and Greek and who also are inerrant interpreters. All of this, I suggest, is a heady brew. And this is why I think you are biting off more than you can chew in advocating inerrancy.

INERRANTIST:

I repeat what I've said before: you are making inerrancy more complicated than it really is.

NON-INERRANTIST:

Not if you give attention to language analysis. I contend that the symbolic and referential nature of words is an issue which inerrantists blissfully ignore.

INERRANTIST:

All I know is that we inerrantists take the Bible *literally.* And if it's an English Bible, that's fine with me. In simple faith I read the Bible, and I take it literally. That's what most inerrantists do. You ought to read some books written by inerrantists which put this point over. For example, you should read *Why I Preach That the Bible Is Literally True* by Dr. W. A. Criswell, pastor of Dallas' First Baptist Church. I can't think of a book which presents in a clearer fashion the way inerrantists believe the Bible and take it literally.

NON-INERRANTIST:

That's interesting. I've read *Why I Preach That the Bible Is Literally True.*

INERRANTIST:

What do you think of it?

NON-INERRANTIST:

I think Dr. Criswell's book does a superb job of demonstrating how inerrantists *don't* take the Bible literally. They reject in practice what they claim in theory.

INERRANTIST:

I challenge you to give me one illustration—just one illustration—of how Dr. Criswell, our articulate spokesman, rejects in practice what he claims in theory.

NON-INERRANTIST:

Turn some time to page 48 of Dr. Criswell's book. Here he rightly observes that chronologists have calculated on the basis of

genealogies in Genesis and in the gospels that the human race—
according to the Bible— appeared on this earth approximately 6,000
years ago. He also rightly acknowledges that human civilization
obviously precedes this date "by many centuries." Thus the Genesis
and gospel genealogies do not support or agree with known anthropological data concerning the age of man. How does Dr. Criswell
"solve" this contradiction? He does so by arguing that "many centuries have intervened" between persons whose names appear in biblical
genealogies. This means, following Criswell's reasoning, that "many
centuries" intervened between the lives of Abraham and Isaac or
between the lives of Isaac and Jacob. "Many centuries" intervened
between Mary's husband Joseph and Jesus. I am not aware of a single
biblical scholar who subscribes to Dr. Criswell's "gap" theory. But that
is neither here nor there. The point I'm making is: Dr. Criswell, noted
inerrantist, rejects in practice what he claims in theory. He claims to
take the Bible literally. But in arguing that "many centuries" intervened between Abraham and Isaac or between Joseph and Jesus, he is
rejecting a literal interpretation and is advocating instead an interpretation which is contrary to the text's literal meaning. Inerrantists don't
practice what they preach.

INERRANTIST:

Say what you want to, inerrantists have sense enough to see that
if you concede that one statement in the Bible is untrue, then maybe
they're all false. Such a concession puts you on a slippery slope I don't
want to slide down.

NON-INERRANTIST:

Then you subscribe to the domino theory. If one domino falls,
maybe they'll all fall; if one statement in the Bible is false, maybe they're
all false.

INERRANTIST:
Right.

NON-INERRANTIST:

You're unconvincing. In logic your way of reasoning is known as the "either-or" fallacy—the fallacy of believing you have two choices and *only* two choices. "*Either* all the Bible is true *or* possibly none of it is true." You're under the impression we have those two choices and those two choices only. But those are not our only alternatives. It makes just as much sense to contend that parts of the Bible are true and parts are not true.

INERRANTIST:

There you go again allowing human reason to evaluate the Bible. You've just said: "It makes just as much sense to contend that parts of the Bible are true and parts are not true." This stance is arrogant. It reflects an absence of humility. My approach is: believe *all* the Bible. Value *all* the Bible. Take it *all* on faith.

NON-INERRANTIST:

What's wrong with human reason? Isn't reason, like the gift of sight, an endowment from God? Why shouldn't biblical texts be submitted reverently to the mind's evaluative capacity? Moreover, I can sense that you think your "believe-it-all" view is one of inerrantism's strengths.

INERRANTIST:

You're mighty right it is. Don't question any of the Bible. *Believe it all.*

NON-INERRANTIST:

I must disagree with you. To my mind your "believe-it-all" attitude is one of inerrantism's major weaknesses. It embodies a rectilinear attitude toward the Bible. To inerrantists all parts of the Bible are to be equally valued because all parts are equally inspired. There are no mountains and valleys. Instead, the Bible is a plateau with every verse on the same level. This rectilinear view, I suggest, leads to a trivialization of the biblical tradition. It implies that as much weight should be assigned to the zoologically-mistaken assertion in Leviticus 11:6 and Deuteronomy 14:7 that the rabbit chews the cud as should be assigned to Jesus' Golden Rule ("Treat other people as you want them to treat you"). Does the Golden Rule, Jesus' summary of the Law of Moses, and an observation about the rabbit's digestive system have equal weight in Christian theology? Or should Christians, mesmerized by inerrantism, expend mental energy attempting to believe or to rationalize the erroneous biblical claim that the hare is a ruminant? Attempts back in the nineteenth century "to explain away" this ruminant claim prompted the doggerel:

> The bishops all have sworn to shed their blood
> To prove 'tis true the hare doth chew the cud.
> O' bishops, doctors, and divines, beware—
> Weak is the faith that hangs upon a hare.

This frequently-quoted doggerel broaches a valid insight: weak—very weak—is a faith which stands or falls on a rabbit's digestive system. Yet to you inerrantists this trivial issue is a matter of life and death. The inerrantism postulate demands that rabbits be ruminants—a zoological impossibility.

INERRANTIST:

Instead of pondering further a rabbit's digestive system, a topic which seems to hold infinite fascination for non-inerrantists, I suggest we look backward across two millenia of church tradition and contemplate again the assertion of II Timothy 3:16, "All scripture is given by inspiration of God, and is profitable for doctrine, for reproof, for correction, for instruction in righteousness." Rabbits or no rabbits, these words—as far as I'm concerned—*prove* the Bible is infallible. Non-inerrantists can't get around II Timothy 3:16–words scores of Christians have read and valued.

NON-INERRANTIST:

I've already told you I don't think II Timothy 3:16 means what you think it means. But—for the sake of our discussion—let's suppose it does. Let's suppose II Timothy 3:16 claims that an English Bible consisting of sixty-six books is inerrant.

INERRANTIST:

Which is precisely what I think it means. Inspiration guarantees inerrancy—regardless of the language.

NON-INERRANTIST:

And so you inerrantists argue: The Bible is inerrant because II Timothy 3:16 says it is inerrant.

INERRANTIST:

You're right. That's our argument.

NON-INERRANTIST:

Is that argument a good one?

INERRANTIST:

Sure it is.

NON-INERRANTIST:

I have my doubts.

INERRANTIST:

That's ridiculous. What stronger argument could you think up than to base a belief in inerrancy on what the Bible claims for itself? Why would you quibble with an argument like that?

NON-INERRANTIST:

Because it's what philosophers or logicians call an argument in a circle. Or to use another expression—question-begging. Begging the question occurs when you assume in an argument's premises the very thing you're pretending to prove. I'll illustrate how a circular argument works. Follow—for a moment—this line of reasoning:

First Premise: The world's best hamburgers are sold in Chicago's hamburger restaurants.
Second Premise: Harold's Hamburger Restaurant is in Chicago.
Conclusion: Therefore, Harold's Hamburger Restaurant sells the world's best hamburgers.

This argument's conclusion "circles back" and merely repeats ideas already present in the premises. Within the context of this line of reasoning the conclusion is valid, but this doesn't mean for one moment that it is true or squares with reality. Maybe the world's best hamburgers are not sold in Chicago's hamburger restaurants. Maybe some Chicago hamburger restaurants serve *lousy* hamburgers. And for the sake of argument, maybe the world's best hamburgers *in fact* are sold in San Francisco. Thus a hamburger skeptic could come along and say, "I don't accept your conclusion about Harold's hamburgers because I don't accept as true the premises upon which it is based." Inerrantists use a similar circular argument when they attempt "to prove" inerrancy by quoting the Bible. Inerrantists reason like this:

First Premise: According to II Timothy 3:16, all statements in the Bible are inspired.
Second Premise: All inspired statements are inerrant.
Conclusion: Therefore, all statements in the Bible are inerrant because all are inspired.

You inerrantists think this line of reasoning "proves" inerrantism. But here's the problem: your conclusion "circles back" and simply repeats ideas found in the argument's premises. You've begged the question. A non-inerrantist could come along and say, "I disagree with the argument's premises. They're faulty. The attempt to make II Timothy 3:16 refer to *all* the Bible—which is a diverse and complex anthology rather than a literary unity—is arbitrary and indefensible. Moreover, inspiration does not necessarily entail inerrancy. Indeed, inerrancy and inspiration are not correlatives. A person can believe in the Bible's inspiration without accepting the postulate of inerrancy."

INERRANTIST:

Circular or not, that's the way we reason. We quote the Bible. That's good enough for me.

NON-INERRANTIST:

On reflection, there're few statements in the Bible which inerrantists can quote to defend their position. There's II Timothy 3:16 and two or three others. That's it. The Bible is remarkably reserved in the claims it makes for itself. It's not a boastful book. Maybe that's why inerrantists constantly feel compelled to pay it theological compliments—some of them extravagant. Instead of paying it theological compliments, why don't you accept the Bible's human side and view its human side as a strength or virtue?

INERRANTIST:

I'd rather pay the Bible theological compliments than to go around spotlighting its "errors" as you non-inerrantists do. All you do is talk about problems, mistakes, discrepancies. You're out to give the Bible a bad image. Or a bad name. And you're out to destroy people's faith.

NON-INERRANTIST:

What you've just said brings into focus a misconception which people have of non-inerrantists. Some people think that non-inerrantists, particularly seminary professors, walk around holding mental microscopes and magnifying glasses in their hands while fervently looking for mistakes in the Bible. Nothing could be further from the truth. We non-inerrantists value the Bible. Many of us have devoted our professional lives to attempting to understand its text and message. We've spent years studying biblical languages, and we view the Bible as indispensable for the Christian faith. It is a literary record of God's revelatory deeds. Inerrantists, unfortunately, have confused God's revelatory deeds with the written record of those deeds—the Bible. They erroneously think that if you question some detail of the biblical record, you're thereby trying to deny or belittle the deeds to which the Bible attests. But this is not the case.

Moreover, by adopting the inerrancy postulate, by arguing that the Bible is completely void of problematic passages, and by insisting that others agree with them, inerrantists have backed non-inerrantists into a corner not of their choosing. Inerrantists come along and say to us, "Either you non-inerrantists agree with us or we'll destroy you." If inerrantists had a "live-and-let-live" attitude, then I'd say: "Three cheers! Let the inerrantists believe as they believe, let the non-inerrantists believe as they believe, and let us all rejoice therein!" But that's not the way it is. Many inerrantists, I've observed, have bully mentalities which compel them to impose their views on others. Thus non-inerrantists have no choice but to respond to inerrantists' aggressive tactics. Our behavior is motivated by a desire to deliver fellow believers from the ideological cul-de-sac down which inerrantists want everyone to travel. That's precisely what inerrantism is—a hermeneutical dead-end street which leads to intellectual dishonesty and to an ignoring of the phenomena of the text. And inerrantists are herding people down this dead-end street because of their distrust of the historical-critical method. To them this method is poison. It undermines their simplistic belief in an infallible Bible. Their adopted strategy is: "Since we can't conquer the historical-critical method or disprove its conclusions, we shall banish its messengers. Fire them from their jobs and drive them into exile." But—paraphrasing Lucretius—what is one person's poison is another person's food. For scores of Christians the historical-critical method has been a blessing. It has enabled them to remain Christians without committing intellectual suicide. It has provided a way for understanding the duplicate accounts, discrepancies, and anachronisms which are encountered in the biblical materials. Maybe Thomas Paine would not have written *The Age of Reason* if he had lived long enough to encounter the historical-critical method. In contrast to non-inerrantists, inerrantists do mental backflips and somersaults attempting to explain away biblical discrepancies, anachronisms, and duplicate accounts. In striving to explain away every problematic statement they alienate from the church people with inquisitive minds, and they impress others as being sophists—devotees to specious reasoning. And what makes the mental contortions of inerrantists so curious is that these mental contortions are unnecessary. The Christian faith does not require an inerrant Bible.

INERRANTIST:

That's where you're wrong. The Christian faith, I believe, *does* require an inerrant Bible.

NON-INERRANTIST:

Why does the Christian faith *require* an inerrant Bible? The Old Testament, which composes more than three-fourths of the Bible, is *not* Christian literature. It's Jewish from Genesis to Malachi. Moreover, every word in the Old Testament was written years before the Christian religion appeared on the scene. How could Christianity "stand or fall" on the basis of anterior non-Christian literature? That's one of the most puzzling ideas inerrantists have. And by the way, have you ever discussed inerrancy with a rabbi? After all is said and done, rabbis know more about the Old Testament—they call it *Tanakh*—than you and I do. It's their Holy Scripture. I've had rabbis, graduates of Hebrew Union in Cincinnati, tell me that if they *had* to be inerrantists, they'd leave the rabbinate. To them inerrantism is a joke.

INERRANTIST:

It may be a joke to them but it's no joke to me. Without an inerrant Bible the Christian religion is in trouble.

NON-INERRANTIST:

A statement like that sends me up the wall. The Christian faith spread across the Roman empire and displaced both Greek and Roman religion *without* a New Testament. When Paul preached to the Athenians and journeyed to Rome to defend the faith before the emperor, he *didn't* have a New Testament to read from. He proclaimed Jesus crucified and raised from the dead—not biblical inerrancy. So I ask this question: if it is true that the Christian religion "stands or falls" on an inerrant Bible, why did our faith spread like prairie fire across the Mediterranean world prior to the Bible's existence? You inerrantists have sold yourselves a bill of goods. You're guilty of Bible worship. You've done to Holy Scripture what Muslims have done to the Koran. You've made it a fetish.

INERRANTIST:

But inerrantism works. It gives people something to stand on. There's nothing as satisfying as holding in hand a Bible and believing you're clutching an infallible, divine revelation. True from beginning to end, *inerrant* in every statement it makes.

NON-INERRANTIST:

I intuit in what you're saying a craving for certainty, an unwillingness to agree with St. Paul that now we see in a glass darkly. Indeed, a characteristic of most inerrantists, I've observed, is an unwillingness to accept human finitude.

INERRANTIST:

By now I think it's obvious you and I don't agree. And I sense we'll never agree.

NON-INERRANTIST:

Maybe you're right. But at least we've exchanged ideas. We must remember we're experiencing today the same controversy experienced a half-century ago by northern denominations. Harry Emerson Fosdick was a warrior in that controversy. Time and again he observed, "Astronomy changes but the stars remain." Through this remark Fosdick was suggesting that the mysteries of the Christian faith hold steady although our ways of understanding those mysteries change. For Christians the ultimate mystery is God's deed in Jesus. There was a time when some Christians thought the record of God's deed in Jesus was conveyed by means of an inerrant Bible. This, we now know, was an erroneous view. But inerrancy's collapse does not diminish God's deed in Jesus. "Astronomy changes but the stars remain." Maybe today's inerrancy controversy is evidence of how some denominations are isolated from the rest of Christendom. Eastern Orthodoxy never believed in inerrancy. Mainline Protestant Churches abandoned inerrancy generations ago. The Roman Catholic Church is in the process of abandoning inerrancy. But some of today's inerrantists are spoiling for an inerrancy fight. They remind me of Japanese soldiers I read about who turn up from time to time in remote areas of the Pacific. Still fighting the Second World War, these soldiers—jungle isolated—are unaware Japan lost the war years ago. Similarly, the inerrancy war was fought in this century's opening decades and inerrantists lost. And lost decisively. Everyone knows this except today's inerrantists who live in intellectual backwaters and have a craving for a simplistic theology which is no longer possible.

INERRANTIST:

Frankly, I find your views elitist. We inerrantists have just begun to fight. And I believe the future belongs to us.

NON-INERRANTIST:

Possibly the *immediate* future *does* belong to you. In a debate the side with popular slogans and the side defending a simplistic view which has mass appeal always has the advantage. But a century or two from now denominations which are today mesmerized with inerrantism will recognize its fallaciousness. And in the life of the church what's one or two centuries? They're a chronological snap of the fingers.

BYSTANDER:

I've listened to your debate with interest, and it's evident the two of you don't see eye to eye. At times a bystander can see dimensions to a controversy which those involved in the controversy don't see. If you'll allow me, I'd like to express one or two thoughts which have crossed my mind as you've debated one another.

INERRANTIST:

Say anything you want to say.

BYSTANDER:

I want to direct my words primarily to non-inerrantist. I sense in your remarks a cerebral approach to the Christian faith. My conjecture is that you're a person who revels in study and in ideas.

NON-INERRANTIST:

To be candid, I do. I love books and the studying of books.

BYSTANDER:

That's fine. And obviously you've read a lot. You've cultivated an inquisitive, intellectual approach to the Christian faith. But is your cerebral version of Christianity palatable or understandable to others? As you were debating, I noted some of the words, expressions, and names you used. You employed expressions like *argumentum ad populum, par excellence,* and circular argument. You discoursed on the referential nature of words and used terms like hermeneutics, rectilinear, anachronism, fetish, and finitude. You referred to Lucretius and to Bishop Athanasius of Alexandria. You made passing reference to the Council of Trent and to literary works like the *Shepherd of Hermas, Tobit,* and *Ecclesiasticus.* How many housewives in Kentucky or shoe salesmen in Texas or dairy farmers in Alabama do you think understand these terms and names? My guess is: *very few do.* Some of you non-inerrantists live in a thought-world inhabited by a small number of people. You talk over people's heads.

NON-INERRANTIST:

That may be true, but—like a rabbi—I view study as a form of worship. We are supposed to worship God not only with our hearts, souls, and strength, but also with our minds.

BYSTANDER:

I agree that God should be worshipped with the mind. But I'm calling your attention to a problem which—quite frankly—I don't think non-inerrantists see. You don't perceive that many rank-and-file Christians are not academically or educationally equipped to follow your line of reasoning. Not for one moment am I suggesting rank-and-file Christians are thick-skulled. To the contrary, they have good minds. They have acquired specialized skills. Some are lawyers. Others are automobile mechanics. Still others are nurses or school teachers. You and I could not begin to match their specialized skills. But they have not devoted years to language study, to manuscript research, or to an examination of early Christian origins as you, a non-inerrantist, have done. Consequently, you speak a language and move in a thought-world they don't understand and shouldn't be expected to understand. Moreover, they have prejudices—prejudices in the sense of prejudgments—about the Bible and how it should be evaluated. Because of these prejudices your non-inerrantist remarks sound threatening to them. Thus I urge you to be sensitive to people's prejudices. And I urge you to remember what Socrates said to the Athenian jury: "Great prejudices cannot be banished in a moment."

NON-INERRANTIST:

People need to examine their prejudgments because their prejudgments can be wrong.

BYSTANDER:

This may well be the case. But the people who hold them don't think they're wrong. Indeed, prejudgments—although erroneous—are frequently hallowed by tradition. That's why they should never be dealt with contemptuously. I've observed that some non-inerrantists—particularly those who live in academic communities—deal condescendingly with inerrantists and their beliefs. They refer to their beliefs as being provincial, and they refer to inerrantists by pejorative terms like "funDAMN-mentalists" and "funny-mentalists." By so doing non-inerrantists (who frequently like to be thought of as being moderate or liberal) reveal there is little moderation among moderates and scant liberalism among liberals. Inerrantists resent this condescending, snobbish treatment, and they lash back. In lashing back they validate the proverb: "Treat people like mules and they act like mules."

INERRANTIST:

You're right. Non-inerrantists treat us like we're a bunch of mules.

BYSTANDER:

We must remember, however, that inerrantists can be rough in the way they deal with non-inerrantists. I've heard inerrantist clergymen refer to non-inerrantists as *skunks* and *infidels*. Yet when you come to know non-inerrantist pastors and seminary professors, you discover that most are devout people who have a high view of Holy Scripture and are personally committed to the Christian faith. Out of a sense of Christian commitment they have devoted their lives to a meticulous and demanding study of the Bible. They "get into trouble" because they refuse to substitute credulity for faith. And they refuse to capitulate to what William Ernest Hocking once designated as one of religion's primary mistakes—the tendency to engage in an "excess of affirmation."

By this phrase ("an excess of affirmation") Hocking was referring to the tendency of religious spokesmen to *claim too much*. They overstate the case and engage in "holy hyperbole." At times this inclination toward an excess of affirmation leads to intellectual dishonesty. Resisting this inclination, non-inerrantists refuse to subscribe to the doctrine of biblical inerrancy. This refusal does not mean they have a "low" or deprecatory attitude toward the Bible. To the contrary, non-inerrantists view the biblical writings as crucial for the Christian religion. They are indispensable because the only way we can learn about past events is by heeding eyewitness accounts of those events. Thus the only way we can learn about pre-Christian Jewish history and religious experience is by heeding eyewitness accounts of that history and religious experience. And the only way we can learn about Jesus' life and about early Christian origins is by heeding eye-witness accounts of Jesus' life and early Christian experience. These accounts are found in that anthology of Jewish and Christian writings called the *Bible. Non-inerrantists believe these accounts, essential for understanding the Christian faith, were written under divine compulsion and have been providentially preserved.* As a result of manuscript research they are aware that the Bible is by far the *best preserved document* which has come down to the modern world from the Middle Eastern and Greco-Roman world of two thousand years ago. *Moreover, non-inerrantists are convinced the Bible is replete with solid historical data and with profound moral and religious insights.* But they are also aware that it has a human side. To deny this human side would be (at least for non-inerrantists) a demeaning exercise in mental bankruptcy. Knowing what they know, non-inerrantists would feel like Elmer Gantrys if they engaged in an "excess of affirmation" by claiming the Bible was completely void of problematic statements. To make this claim, a claim which they regard as being theologically unnecesssary, would be for non-inerrantists a resurrecting of the ghost of William Jennings Bryan and a revitalizing of the atmosphere which surrounded the Scopes trial. In fact, non-inerrantists find the contemporary Donnybrook over biblical inerrancy to be an embarrassment, a reversion to the ludicrous anti-intellectualism of Billy Sunday's era.

Before we part company, let me add one final word. One of you is an inerrantist. The other is a non-inerrantist. You're both capitulating to gnosticism, Christendom's oldest heresy which contends that the Christian life consists essentially of right belief. You're hooked on the idea that the Christian faith is a complex of doctrines on topics like inerrancy. In reality, the Christian faith is a continuing existential response to God's momentous deed in Jesus. Both of you, I suggest, should fall to your knees and ask God's forgiveness for becoming *de facto* gnostics.

CHAPTER FOUR

❦

John Stuart Mill
and the
Inerrancy Controversy

John Stuart Mill was a nineteenth-century Englishman who for thirty-five years was an official with the East India Company. He was also a lay philosopher. In 1859 he published an essay which has become a philosophical classic. The essay is titled *On Liberty*. It deals with the tendency of governments "to bully" citizens who hold unpopular views. Time and again throughout history, John Stuart Mill contended, governments–exercising their collective authority over individuals–have interfered with people's beliefs. Particularly have they interfered with unpopular views held by disliked minorities. John Stuart Mill argued that governments should abandon their tendency to trample on an unpopular minority's beliefs. Rather, he contended, unpopular views should be discussed and scrutinized.

On Liberty, I concede, is an essay which deals primarily with political (not with religious) dissent. Yet its line of reasoning is also applicable to religious controversies. Thus in this chapter I want to apply John Stuart Mill's argumentation in *On Liberty* to today's inerrancy controversy.

First of all, Mr. Mill in his essay contended that unpopular ideas or beliefs should not be suppressed because their suppression *can result in a blotting out of truth*. An unconventional opinion or a disliked view may ultimately turn out to be true. An idea's unpopularity does *not necessarily* signify the idea is false; contrariwise, an idea's popularity does *not necessarily* signify the idea is true. The divine right of kings, the flat-earth hypothesis, Ptolemaic astronomy, feudalism, infanticide, slavery, gladiatorial combats, religious persecution, inferiority of women, racial segregation, the glorification of war: all were once popular viewpoints and practices subscribed to by the masses. An Athenian majority, we must remember, approved Socrates' execution. On the other hand, the Christian religion, Beethoven's symphonies, printing, women's suffrage, anesthesiological research, and Copernican astronomy share a common feature: originally all were unpopular. Yet they are accepted today. History is replete with examples of previously persecuted opinions and practices which are now approved. Thus no viewpoint—regardless of how unpopular it is—should be denied public scrutiny and debate. Public scrutiny and debate are necessary in order to make possible the survival of unconventional views which ultimately are shown to be correct.

The principle of not persecuting (or suppressing) a viewpoint *because ultimately it may prove to be right* applies to the inerrancy controversy. Taking the long view, non-inerrantist opinions (unpopular with the rank-and-file) may turn out to be correct. This possibility suggests these views should not be suppressed. Instead, they should be discussed, analyzed, debated. In this debate inerrantists cannot lose. If non-inerrantism's view of scripture is disproven and inerrantism's view is substantiated, then inerrantism will have carried the day. If non-inerrantism's view of scripture is shown to be correct, then inerrantists will have been delivered from an illusion.

In *On Liberty* John Stuart Mill went further and advanced a second reason for not suppressing unpopular views—a reason having to do with the confirming of truth. He reasoned as follows. Grant—for the sake of argument—that an unpopular view is false. Should this unpopular position be suppressed because of its falsity? The answer again is *no! Unpopular positions, although false, should not be suppressed because ultimately truth is served through the refuting of false views.* Disproving erroneous beliefs provides devotees of true beliefs an opportunity to rethink why they believe as they do. This rethinking process is good because viewpoints not constantly reexamined tend to become stale; contrariwise, rethinking beliefs keeps them vibrant.

This line of reasoning applies to today's inerrancy controversy. Grant—for the sake of argument—that seminary professors, pastors, and lay Christians who reject biblical inerrancy are *wrong*. Their wrongness does not mean their views should be suppressed. Instead, inerrantists should energetically explore why non-inerrantists believe as they do. They should expose and disprove the "false, unpopular" beliefs held by non-inerrantists. By so doing, inerrantists will confirm their inerrantism. Inerrantism's "truth" will be served and strengthened by refuting non-inerrantism's "error."

Pursuing John Stuart Mill's contention that unpopular viewpoints (like non-inerrancy) should not be suppressed but should be examined, I will now cite two hundred questions which are based on biblical texts. These inquiries are the kind which non-inerrantists confront; they are also the kind which inerrantists tend to ignore. I ask you, the reader, to ponder them. Do these questions and the credibility-or-morality issues they raise support or undermine the inerrancy theory? In light of these questions, should inerrancy (a popular viewpoint) be swallowed hook-line-and- sinker? And in light of these questions, should non-inerrancy (an unpopular viewpoint) be rejected as untenable? The two hundred questions are:

1. *A Question Concerning the Phrase "One Flesh"*

The creation story in Genesis 2 concludes with the words, "Therefore a man leaves his father and mother and cleaves to his wife, and they become *one flesh*" (Genesis 2:24). In Matthew 19:5 Jesus quotes this *one flesh* statement to defend marriage's sacred indissolubility. However, in I Corinthians 6:16 Paul cites this *one flesh* statement as proof of the evil of prostitution. How logically can the *same* Genesis statement about a man and a woman becoming *one flesh* (Genesis 2:24) refer *both to marriage's holy indissolubility* (as it does in Matthew 19:5) *and to sexual intercourse with a prostitute* (as it does in I Corinthians 6:16)?

2. *A Question About Enoch*

Genesis 5:1-18 preserves the tradition that Adam was the father of Seth (5:3), who was the father of Enosh (5:6), who was the father of Kenan

(5:9), who was the father of Mahalalel (5:12), who was the father of Jared (5:15), who was the father of Enoch (5:18). Thus Genesis 5:1-18 asserts that Enoch was the *sixth* descendant after Adam. This sixth-descendant tradition is found also in Luke 3:37-38. Jude 14, however, states that Enoch was the seventh descendant after Adam. Was Enoch the *sixth* descendant after Adam (as Genesis 5:1-18 and Luke 3:37-38 report), or was Enoch the *seventh* descendant after Adam (as Jude 14 states)?

3. *A Question Concerning Abraham's Departure From Haran*
A reading of Genesis 11:26 and Genesis 12:4 reveals the following biographical data:

a. Terah was *70 years old* when his son Abraham was born (Genesis 11:26).
b. Abraham was *75 years old* when he left Haran (his father's city) for "the promised land" (Genesis 12:4).

A combining of these two biographical facts means that Terah (Abraham's father) was *145 years old* when Abraham left Haran for "the promised land". Moreover, Genesis 11:32 reports that Terah was *205 years old* when he died in Haran. This means that Abraham left Haran (his father's city) *60 years before* his father (Terah) died. Yet Acts 7:4 quotes Stephen, the first Christian martyr, as stating that Abraham did not leave Haran until *after* Terah's death. Did Abraham leave the city of Haran *sixty years before* his father's death (as Genesis 11:26, 11:32, and 12:4 inform us), or did he leave the city of Haran *after* his father's death (as Stephen informs us in Acts 7:4)?

4. *A Question Concerning the Oak of Moreh*
Was the oak of Moreh located at *Gilgal* (as Deuteronomy 11:29-31 states), or was it located at *Shechem* (as Genesis 12:5-7 asserts)?

5. *A Question Concerning Joseph and the Ishmaelites*
Genesis 37:25-27 reports that Joseph was sold to the Ishmaelites *by his*

brothers. This tradition is repeated in Genesis 45:4-5. Yet Genesis 37:28 asserts Joseph was lifted out of a pit and sold to the Ishmaelites *by Midianite traders.* Was Joseph sold into slavery *by his brothers,* or was he sold into slavery *by Midianites?*

6. *A Question Concerning Abraham*
Exodus 6:2-3 asserts that God *did not* reveal his personal name *Yahweh* to Abraham. However, Genesis 15:7-8 asserts that God *did* reveal himself to Abraham as Yahweh. *Did* God or *did* God *not* reveal himself as Yahweh to Abraham?

7. *A Question Concerning Isaac*
Exodus 6:2-3 asserts that God did *not* reveal his personal name *Yahweh* to Isaac. How, therefore, was Isaac able to call upon the name of *Yahweh* (as reported in Genesis 26:23-25)?

8. *A Question Concerning Jacob*
Exodus 6:2-3 asserts that God *did not* reveal his personal name *Yahweh* to Jacob. However, Genesis 28:10-17 asserts that God *did* reveal himself to Jacob as Yahweh. *Did* God or *did* God *not* reveal himself as Yahweh to Jacob?

9. *A Question Concerning the Egyptian Sojourn*
Did the Jews remain in Egypt for *400 years* (as Acts 7:6 and Genesis 15:13 report), or did the Jews remain in Egypt for *430 years* (as Exodus 12:40-41 reports)?

10. *A Question Concerning the Digging of the Beersheba Well*
Was the well at Beersheba dug *by Abraham* (as Genesis 21:30 reports), or was it dug *by Isaac's servants* (as Genesis 26:32 reports)?

11. *A Question Concerning the Bethel Memorial Stone*
Did Jacob give the name *Bethel* to the memorial stone at Luz while making a journey *to* Paddan-aram (as recounted in Genesis 28:19), or

did he give the name *Bethel* to the memorial stone at Luz many years later while journeying home *from* Paddan-aram (as recounted in Genesis 35:14-15)?

12. *A Question Concerning Changing Jacob's Name*
Was Jacob's name changed to "Israel" after the *wrestling episode at Peniel* (as reported in Genesis 32:22-32), or was Jacob's name changed to "Israel" *after the epiphany episode at Bethel* (as reported in Genesis 35:5-15)?

13. *A Question About Jacob's Corpse and Burial Place*
Jacob was the grandson of Abraham and the father of Joseph. According to Genesis 50:12-14, Joseph buried Jacob's corpse in the *cave of Machpelah* (to the east of Mamre) which Abraham had bought from Ephron the Hittite. Contrarily, Acts 7:15-16 observes that Jacob was buried *in a tomb at Shechem* which Abraham had bought from the sons of Hamor. Was Jacob entombed in the *cave of Machpelah* (as Genesis 50:12-14 reports), or was Jacob entombed at *Shechem* (as Stephen reports in Acts 7:15-16)? Was Jacob's burial place purchased from *Ephron the Hittite* (Genesis 50:12-14), or was it purchased from the *sons of Hamor* (Acts 7:15-16)?

14. *A Question Concerning Moses' Father-in-Law*
Was Moses' father-in-law a man named *Jethro* the priest of Midian (as reported in Exodus 3:1), or was Moses' father-in-law a man named *Hobab* the son of Reuel the Midianite (as reported in Numbers 10:29)? Or was Moses' father-in-law a man named *Reuel* (as reported in Exodus 2:15-22)?

15. *A Question Concerning Moses' Oratorical Skills*
Exodus 4:10 quotes Moses as saying, "Oh, my Lord, I am not eloquent, either heretofore or since thou hast spoken to thy servant; but I am slow of speech and tongue." To cope with Moses' poor oratorical skills, Aaron (according to Exodus 4:14-17) was chosen to

be Moses' spokesman. Yet according to Acts 7:22 Moses was a man "mighty in his words and deeds." Was Moses an *orator* (as he is described in Acts 7:22), or was he a man *hesitant in speech* (as he is described in Exodus 4:10-17)?

16. *A Question Concerning Boiling the Passover Lamb*

In Deuteronomy 16:1-8 the Jews were commanded by God *to boil* the Passover sacrifice. "And you should boil it and eat it at the place which the Lord your God will choose" (Deuternomy 16:7). Contrarily, in Exodus 12:1-9 the Jews were commanded by God *not to boil but to roast* the Passover sacrifice. "Do not eat any of it raw or boiled with water, but roasted, its head with its legs and its inner part" (Exodus 12:9). Did God command the Passover sacrifice *to be boiled* or *not to be boiled?* Did God command the Passover sacrifice to be *boiled* or to be *roasted?*

17. *A Question Concerning the Golden Calf*

During the wilderness wanderings the Jews made a molten calf to worship. This molten calf was destroyed in anger by Moses. Exodus 32:20 relates that Moses "took the calf which they had made, and burnt it with fire, and ground it to powder, and scattered it upon the water, and made the people of Israel drink it." However, Deuteronomy 9:21 quotes Moses as saying that he took the calf "and burned it with fire and crushed it, grinding it very small, until it was as fine as dust; and I threw the dust of it into the brook that descended out of the mountain." Was the powder from the demolished golden calf mixed with water and drunk by the Israelites (Exodus 32:20), or was the powder from the demolished golden calf thrown into a mountain stream (Deuteronomy 9:21)?

18. *A Question Concerning the Ark of the Covenant*

Exodus 37:1-16 reports that the ark of the covenant was constructed out of acacia wood by an artisan named *Bezalel.* But Deuteronomy 10:1-5 reports that it was constructed out of acacia wood by *Moses.* Was the ark of the covenant constructed by *Moses* (as stated in Deuteronomy 10:1-5), or was it built by *Bezalel* (as stated in Exodus 37:1-16)?

19. *A Question Concerning the Sabbath's Purpose*

What is the Sabbath's purpose? Was the Sabbath made holy to serve as a *rest day* after six days of creation (Exodus 20:8-11), or to serve as a *reminder of Egyptian slavery and the exodus* (Deuteronomy 5:12-15)? In other words, when God gave the fourth commandment, did he say, "In six days I, the Lord, made the earth, the sky, the seas, and everything in them, but on the seventh day I rested. That is why I, the Lord, blessed the Sabbath and made it holy" (Exodus 20:11), or did he say, "Remember that you were slaves in Egypt, and that I, the Lord your God, rescued you by my great power and strength. That is why I command you to observe the Sabbath" (Deuteronomy 5:15)?

20. *A Question Concerning Commandments to Sacrifice*

Jeremiah 7:21-23 asserts that God did *not* command the Jews to offer sacrifices and burnt offerings. Yet numerous passages like Exodus 20:24-26 and Exodus 29 assert that God *did* command the Jews to offer sacrifices and burnt offerings. After leaving Egypt were the Jews given commands to sacrifice (as Exodus 20:24-26 makes clear), or were they *not* given commands to sacrifice (as Jeremiah 7:22 asserts)?

21. *A Question Concerning the Incense Altar's Location*

Was the golden incense altar placed *outside* the Tabernacle veil (as Exodus 40:18-27 asserts), or was it placed *behind* the Tabernacle veil along with the ark of the covenant (as Hebrews 9:2-7 asserts)?

22. *A Question Concerning Insect Legs*

Insects have six legs, and no paleontological evidence suggests that four-legged insects have ever existed. Why does the Mosaic law erroneously refer to four-legged insects (Leviticus 11:20-23)?

23. *A Question Concerning the Camel*
The camel is a cloven-footed creature having two toes on each foot. Why does Leviticus 11:3-4 mistakenly assert that the camel is not cloven-footed?

24. *A Question Concerning the Rock Badger*
The rock badger is an animal which does not chew the cud. Why does Leviticus 11:5 mistakenly classify the rock badger (also known as the coney or the Syrian hyrax) as a cud chewer?

25. *A Question Concerning the Rabbit*
The rabbit does not chew the cud. Why does Leviticus 11:6 mistakenly classify the rabbit as a cud chewer (a ruminant mammal classification no zoologist would accept)?

26. *A Question Concerning the Bat*
The bat is not a bird. It is a featherless, hairy mammal. Why is the bat (a featherless, hairy mammal) erroneously classified as a bird in Leviticus 11:19?

27. *A Question About Corpse Touching*
Did the Lord tell Moses that a person who touches a corpse is ritually unclean *until sundown* (as reported in Leviticus 22:4-7), or did the Lord tell Moses that a person who touches a corpse is ritually unclean *for seven days* (as reported in Numbers 19:11-12)?

28. *A Question Concerning the Tribe of Levi*
Did God command Moses *to number* the Levi tribe (as reported in Numbers 3:14-15), or did God command Moses *not to number* the Levi tribe (as reported in Numbers 1:49)?

29. *A Question About the Carrying Poles*
Were the carrying poles for the ark of the covenant *to remain*

permanently in their rings (as Exodus 25:13-15 states), or *were they periodically to be removed and then reinserted* (as Numbers 4:5-6 suggests)?

30. *A Question About the Levites*
Does the Old Testament teach that the Levites entered priestly service at age *twenty* (as reported in I Chronicles 23:24-30) or at age *twenty-five* (as reported in Numbers 8:23-24) or at age *thirty* (as reported in Numbers 4:2-3)?

31. *A Question Concerning Aaron's Death*
Aaron was Moses' brother who died during the wilderness wanderings. Deuteronomy 10:6 states that Aaron died and was buried at a place named *Moserah*. Contrarily, Numbers 20:28 states that Aaron died at a place named *Mt. Hor*, a mountain on the border of the land of Edom (Numbers 20:23). According to Numbers 33:31-37, *Mt. Hor* was the seventh stop or encampment made by the Jews after leaving *Moserah* during their wilderness wanderings. Thus did Aaron—Moses' brother—die and undergo burial at *Moserah* (as Deuteronomy 10:6 states) or did he die seven encampments later at *Mt. Hor* (as Numbers 20:28 states)?

32. *A Question Concerning Twelve Stones*
Twelve stones were set up to commemorate the Israelites' crossing the Jordan River. Joshua 4:9 reports these stones were set up in the river ("And Joshua set up twelve stones in the midst of the Jordan, in the place where the feet of the priests bearing the ark of the covenant had stood; and they are there to this day"). Contrarily, Joshua 4:20 records that the twelve stones were set up *in Gilgal* ("And those twelve stones, which they took out of the Jordan, Joshua set up in Gilgal"). Was the twelve-stone-memorial erected *in the Jordan River* (as Joshua 4:9 asserts), or was it erected on dry land near Jericho *in Gilgal* (as Joshua 4:20 records)? How could the twelve stones have been erected on land in Gilgal in light of the report of Joshua 4:9 that the twelve stones were in the midst of the Jordan River *to this day*?

33. *A Question concerning Hazor and King Jabin*

Hazor, a Canaanite city, was ruled by King Jabin. Joshua 11:1-11 reports that Joshua and the Israelites destroyed both King Jabin and the city of Hazor. Thus Joshua 11:10-11 reports, "And Joshua turned back at that time, and took Hazor, and smote its king with the sword; for Hazor formerly was the head of all those kingdoms. And they put to the sword all who were in it, utterly destroying them; there was none left that breathed, and he burned Hazor with fire."

Yet Judges 4:1-24, contrarily, reports that Deborah and the Israelites destroyed Jabin, King of Hazor.

Who destroyed Jabin, the Canaanite king? Was he destroyed *by Joshua* during the Israelite conquest (as Joshua 11:10-11 asserts), or was he destroyed decades later during the era of the Judges *by Deborah* (as Judges 4:24 reports)? How could *Jabin* be *king of Hazor* during the era of the Judges in light of the fact that he had been *killed* decades earlier by Joshua who *destroyed the city of Hazor*?

34. *A Question Concerning Food*

Does the Bible teach that *some foods are unfit* for human consumption (as Leviticus 11 and Deuteronomy 14 assert), or does the Bible teach that *all foods are fit* for human consumption (as Mark 7:19 asserts)?

35. *A Question Concerning the Conquest*

In the 1300s B.C. the Jews invaded Palestine under Joshua's leadership. Joshua 11:16-23 contends that this conquest was *total*. For example, Joshua 11:16-17 states, "So Joshua took *all that land*, the hill country and the lowland and the Arabah and the hill country of Israel and its lowland from Mount Halak, that rises toward Seir, as far as Baalgad in the valley of Lebanon below Mount Herman. And he took *all their kings* and smote them and put them to death." Contrarily, passages like Joshua 13:1-7 and Judges 1:19-35 list in considerable detail areas of Palestine which the Jews did not conquer during the conquest. Was Joshua's conquest of the promised land *total* (as Joshua

11:16-23 boasts), or was the conquest *partial* and *fragmentary* (as Joshua 13:1-7 and Judges 1:19-35 concede)?

36. *A Question Concerning the King of Hebron*

Joshua 10 deals with the Jewish conquest of Palestine. The *king of Hebron* (Joshua 10:5 and 10:16) was one of five Amorite kings who hid in the cave of Makkedah and *was slaughtered* by Joshua and the men of Israel (as related in Joshua 10:26). However, Joshua 10:36-37 relates that shortly thereafter Joshua and all Israel went up from Eglon to Hebron and *killed the king of Hebron* and every person in it. How was it possible for Joshua during the conquest *to kill* (Joshua 10:26) and then to *rekill* (Joshua 10:36-37) the king of Hebron?

37. *A Question Concerning the City of Hebron*

During the conquest how did Caleb manage to capture the city of Hebron and *drive out its inhabitants* (as Joshua 15:13-14 relates) in light of the fact that shortly before the city had been destroyed by Joshua and *its inhabitants exterminated* (as Joshua 10:36-37 relates)?

38. *A Question Concerning the City of Dan*

Judges 18:27-29 reports that the Jews burned and rebuilt the city of Laish. Having been rebuilt, the city was given the new name of *Dan*. This burning, rebuilding, and renaming took place during the era of the Judges, which lasted from approximately 1200 B.C. to 1000 B.C. Genesis 14:14, however, reports that Abraham (who lived around 1750 B.C.) pursued Lot's captors to the city of Dan. How was Abraham able to pursue Lot's captors to the city of Dan (as reported in Genesis 14:14) in view of the historical fact that the city of Dan did not come into existence until *several centuries later* (as reported in Judges 18:29)? In other words, how was Abraham able to pursue Lot's captors to a city (Dan) which did not exist in Abraham's time?

39. *A Question Concerning the Monarchy's Establishment*

Was God *in favor* of establishing the monarchy in Israel (as the ninth and tenth chapters of I Samuel make clear), or was God *opposed* to establishing the monarchy in Israel (as the eighth chapter of I Samuel makes clear)?

40. *A Question Concerning King Saul*

Was Saul proclaimed king of the Jews *at Mizpah* (as I Samuel 10:17-24 reports), or was he proclaimed king of the Jews *at Gilgal* (as I Samuel 11:15 reports)?

41. *A Question Concerning Goliath*

Goliath was a Philistine giant who was a "military threat" to the Jews. According to I Samuel 17:1-51, Goliath was slain *by David* with a sling. Yet according to II Samuel 21:19, Goliath was killed by *Elhanan the Bethlehemite*. Did *David* kill Goliath (as reported in I Samuel 17:1-51), or did *Elhanan the Bethlehemite* slay Goliath (as reported in II Samuel 21:19)?

42. *A Question Concerning King David's Sons Born in Jerusalem*

Two lists appear in the Old Testament of King David's sons born in Jerusalem. They are as follows:

The Thirteen-Name List Found in I Chronicles 3:5-7	*The Eleven-Name List Found in II Samuel 5:13-16*
Shimea	Shammua
Shobab	Shobab
Nathan	Nathan
Solomon	Solomon
Ibhar	Ibhar
Elishama	
Eliphelet	Eliphelet
Nogah	
Nepheg	Nepheg
Japhia	Japhia

Elishama	Elishama
Eliada	Eliada
Eliphelet	
	Elishua

The list in I Chronicles contains the name of *Nogah*, the II Samuel list does *not*. The I Chronicles list contains 13 names; the II Samuel list contains 11 names. Did King David have a son named *Nogah*? Did King David father 11 or 13 sons while living in Jerusalem?

Moreover, the list in I Chronicles has *two* sons named *Elishama* and *Eliphelet* whereas the list in II Samuel has one son named *Elishama* and one son named *Eliphelet*. Did David have one son or two sons bearing the names of *Elishama* and *Eliphelet*?

43. *A Question Concerning Hadadezer's Captured Horsemen*
King David defeated in battle Hadadezer, king of Zobah. II Samuel 8:4 observes that David captured *1,700 horsemen* when the battle was over. But I Chronicles 18:4 observes that David captured *7,000 horsemen* when the battle was over. Did David capture *1,700* or *7,000* horsemen belonging to Hadadezer?

44. *A Question Concerning David's Battle With Shobach*
While defeating the Syrian army commanded by Shobach, did David kill *7,000 chariot drivers* and *40,000 foot soldiers* (as reported in I Chronicles 19:18), or did he kill *700 chariot drivers* and *40,000 horsemen* (as reported in II Samuel 10:18)?

45. *A Question Concerning King Saul, Jesse, and David*
I Samuel 16:14-23 relates how David, son of Jesse the Bethlehemite, played a lyre to soothe King Saul when he was tormented by an evil spirit. This passage makes it clear that King Saul and David knew one another. For example, I Samuel 16:23 asserts, "And whenever the evil spirit from God was upon Saul, David took the lyre and played it with his hands; so Saul was refreshed, and was well, and the evil spirit

departed from him." The passage also makes it clear that Jesse, David's father, and King Saul knew one another. For example, Jesse sent gifts (bread, wine, and a kid) to Saul (I Samuel 16:20), and King Saul asked Jesse to allow David to be a court musician (I Samuel 16:22).

When we move from I Samuel 16 to I Samuel 17, we encounter the episode of David's battle with the Philistine giant. After relating David's triumph over Goliath, the text—puzzlingly—states that King Saul did not know David or who David's father was (I Samuel 17:55-58). In view of the fact that Saul knew both David and David's father (I Samuel 16:17-23), why does the text suggest later (I Samuel 17:55-58) that King Saul knew neither David nor David's father?

46. *A Question Concerning David's Census*
King David conducted a census of Israel. II Samuel 24:1 states that *God* commanded David to conduct the census. However, I Chronicles 21:1 states that *Satan* incited David to conduct the census. Did David conduct the census because of *God's influence or because of Satan's influence?*

47. *A Question Concerning the Outcome of David's Census*
Did David's census reveal *800,000 warriors in Israel* and *500,000 warriors in Judah* (as II Samuel 24:9 declares it did), or did David's census reveal *1,100,000 warriors in Israel* and *470,000 warriors in Judah* (as I Chronicles 21:5 declares it did)?

48. *A Question Concerning the Prophet Gad's Message*
Did the Lord instruct the prophet Gad to tell David that his punishment for taking a census of Israel would involve *seven famine years* (as II Samuel 24:13 observes), or did the Lord instruct the prophet Gad to tell David his punishment would involve *three famine years* (as I Chronicles 21:12 observes)?

49. *A Question About Araunah's Threshing Floor*
The prophet Gad instructed King David to purchase a threshing floor

belonging to Araunah (or Ornan) the Jebusite as a place to build an altar. Did David pay *50 silver coins* for the Jebusite threshing place (as reported in II Samuel 24:24), or did he pay *600 gold coins* for the Jebusite threshing place (as reported in I Chronicles 21:25)?

50. *A Question Concerning King Solomon's Horses*
King Solomon owned horses and maintained royal stables. Did King Solomon maintain *4,000 stalls* for his horses (as affirmed in II Chronicles 9:25), or did he maintain *40,000 stalls* for his horses (as affirmed in I Kings 4:26)?

51. *A Question Concerning the Height of Jachin and Boaz*
Jachin and *Boaz* were names given to the twin bronze pillars which stood in Solomon's Temple (I Kings 7:21). I Kings 7:15 states that their height was *18 cubits*. Yet II Chronicles 3:15 states that their height was *35 cubits*. Were Jachin and Boaz *18 cubits high* (as described in I Kings 7:15), or were they *35 cubits high* (as described in II Chronicles 3:15)?

52. *A Question Concerning the Capitals of Jachin and Boaz*
Jachin and *Boaz* were names given to the twin bronze pillars which stood in Solomon's Temple (I Kings 7:21). These pillars had capitals. II Kings 25:17 states these capitals were *three cubits high*. Yet I Kings 7:16 states these capitals were *five cubits high* (a tradition repeated in Jeremiah 52:22). Were the capitals *three cubits in height* or were they *five cubits in height?*

53. *A Question Concerning the Capacity of the Molten Sea*
Solomon's temple was furnished with a molten sea (described in I Kings 7:23-26 and II Chronicles 4:1-6), a vessel in which priests washed. Was the capacity of the molten sea in Solomon's temple *2,000 baths* (as I Kings 7:26 reports), or was the capacity of the molten sea in Solomon's temple *over 3,000 baths* (as II Chronicles 4:5 reports)?

54. *A Question About the Content of the Ark of the Covenant*
I Kings 8:9 observes, "There was nothing in the ark except the *two tables of stone* which Moses put there at Horeb." An identical view about the ark's content is expressed in II Chronicles 5:10. Yet Hebrews 9:4 asserts that the ark of the covenant contained not only the *tables of stone* but also *Aaron's rod that budded* and a *golden urn containing manna*. Did the ark of the covenant contain *only* the *two tables of stone* (as I Kings 8:9 explicitly reports), or did it contain the *two tables of stone, Aaron's rod, and a golden urn containing manna* (as Hebrews 9:4 explicitly reports)?

55. *A Question Concerning Hiram's Mother*
Huramabi (or Huram) was the master craftsman who worked on Solomon's Temple. Was his mother from the *Dan* tribe (as II Chronicles 2:14 reports), or was she from the *Naphtali* tribe (as I Kings 7:14 reports)?

56. *A Question Concerning King Abijam's Maternal Ancestry*
Abijam (or Abijah) was king of Judah. He began reigning in the eighteenth year of King Jeroboam of Israel. I Kings 15:2 observes that Abijam's mother was *Maacah the daughter of Abishalom*. Yet II Chronicles 13:2 observes that Abijam's mother was *Micaiah the daughter of Uriel of Gibeah*. Which tradition is correct? Was King Abijam the son of *Maacah the daughter of Abishalom*, or was he the son of *Micaiah the daughter of Uriel of Gibeah*?

57. *A Question Concerning a Mother*
Abijam and Asa, both kings of Judah, were father and son. How was it possible for both of these men to have the *same mother*—a woman named *Maacah the daughter of Abishalom* (as I Kings 15:1-2 and I Kings 15:9-10 report)?

58. *A Question Concerning Ahaziah's Coronation Age*
Ahaziah, son of Jehoram, was a king of Judah. Was Ahaziah *22 years*

old when he began to reign (as reported in II Kings 8:26), or was he *42 years old* when he began to reign (as reported in II Chronicles 22:2)?

59. *A Question Concerning Ahaziah's Death*
Ahaziah, king of Judah, was murdered at the instigation of Jehu, king of Israel. What were the *circumstances* of King Ahaziah's death? Did he die in Megiddo after having been shot while riding in his chariot up the ascent of Gur (as II Kings 9:27-28 recounts)? Or was Ahaziah executed after hiding out for a time in Samaria (as II Chronicles 22:9 recounts)?

60. *A Question Concerning Joash's Guards*
Did Jehoiada have Joash guarded by *professional soldiers* (as II Kings 11:4-8 relates), or did Jehoiada have Joash guarded by *priests and Levites* (as II Chronicles 23:3-7 relates)?

61. *A Question Concerning King Jehoiachin's Coronation Age*
Jehoiachin was one of the Kingdom of Judah's kings. Was Jehoiachin *eighteen years old* when he became king (as II Kings 24:8 reports), or was he *eight years old* when he became king (as II Chronicles 36: 9 reports)?

62. *A Question Concerning Zedekiah's Relationship to Jehoiachin*
Was Zedekiah Jehoiachin's *uncle* (as reported in II Kings 24:17), or was Zedekiah Jehoiachin's *brother* (as reported in II Chronicles 36:10)?

63. *A Question Concerning Jehoiachin's Reign*
Did King Jehoiachin reign for *three months* (as II Kings 24:8 reports), or did King Jehoiachin reign for *three months and ten days* (as II Chronicles 36:9 reports)?

64. *A Question Concerning Ezra's Enumeration of the Returnees from Babylonian Exile*
Ezra's second chapter contains a listing of clans or families which

returned to Jerusalem from Babylonian exile. The number of returnees in each clan is noted. Ezra 2:64 states that the total number of returned exiles was 42,360. Yet when the various clan numbers listed in Ezra's second chapter are added together, they total 29,818–a difference of 12,542. Why this 12,542 discrepancy?

65. *A Question Concerning Asaph's Descendants*
Did *128 musicians* who were descendants of Asaph return to Jerusalem from Babylonian exile (as Ezra 2:41 states), or did *148 musicians* who were descendants of Asaph return to Jerusalem from Babylonian exile (as Nehemiah 7:44 states)?

66. *A Question Concerning Clan Enumeration in Ezra and Nehemiah*
Ezra 2 and Nehemiah 7 list Jewish clans which returned to Jerusalem from Babylonian exile. In both of these chapters the number of returnees in each clan is noted. Below are three columns. The first column lists ten clans by name. The second column contains the number of returnees for each clan as reported in Ezra 2 while the third column contains the number as reported in Nehemiah 7.

Clan	Ezra 2	Nehemiah 7
Arah	775	652
Bebai	623	628
Pahath Moab	2,812	2,818
Zattu	945	845
Azgad	1,222	2,322
Adonikam	666	667
Adin	454	655
Bigvai	2,056	2,067
Bezai	323	324
Hashum	223	328

A column comparison reveals that in no case do the numbers of returnees in each clan agree. Why do Ezra and Nehemiah have these *ten numerical discrepancies?*

67. *A Question Concerning Nehemiah's Enumeration of the Returnees from Babylonian Exile*

Nehemiah's seventh chapter contains a listing of clans or families which returned to Jerusalem from Babylonian exile. The number of returnees in each clan is noted. Nehemiah 7:66 states that the total number of returned exiles was 42,360. Yet when the various clan numbers listed in Nehemiah's seventh chapter are added together, they total 31,089—a difference of 11,271. Why this 11,271 discrepancy?

68. *A Question Concerning Jesus' Genealogy*

Matthew 1 and Luke 3 contain genealogies which trace Jesus' paternal lineage. These two genealogies, while tracing Jesus' descent from King David to Joseph, read as follows:

Matthew's Genealogy	*Luke's Genealogy*
(Matthew 1:6-17)	*(Luke 3:23-31)*
David	David
Solomon	Nathan
Rehoboam	Mattatha
Abijah	Menna
Asa	Melea
Jehoshaphat	Eliakim
Joram	Jonam
Uzziah	Joseph
Jotham	Judah
Ahaz	Simeon
Hezekiah	Levi
Manasseh	Matthat
Amos	Jorim
Josiah	Eliezer, Jesus, Er
Jechoniah	Elmadam, Cosam, Addi, Melchi, Neri
Shealtiel	*Shealtiel*
Zerubbabel	*Zerubbabel*

Abiud	Rhesa
Eliakim	Joanan
Azor	Joda
Zadok	Josech
Achim	Semein
Eliud	Mattathias, Maath, Naggai,
Eleazar	Esli, Nahum, Amos, Mattathias,
Matthan	Joseph, Jannai, Melchi, Levi
Jacob	Matthat, Heli
Joseph	*Joseph*

Matthew's genealogy from David to Joseph contains approximately 27 names while Luke's genealogy from David to Joseph contains approximately 42 names. Why this numerical difference? Moreover, only four names (note the above italicized names: David, Shealtiel, Zerubbabel, and Joseph) in these genealogies are identical. Which one of these diverse genealogies correctly reflects Jesus' paternal lineage?

69. *A Question Concerning the Temptations*

Matthew 4:1-11 and Luke 4:1-13 contain accounts of Jesus' Satanic temptations. In Matthew the temptation order is: (a) turning stone to bread, (b) casting down from the temple pinnacle, and (c) worshiping Satan. In Luke a different order appears. The Lucan order is: (a) turning stone to bread, (b) worshiping Satan, and (c) casting down from the temple pinnacle. Which *temptation order* is correct?

70. *A Question Concerning Satan's Temptation*

At the beginning of his ministry Jesus was tempted by Satan. One of these temptations involved turning stone into bread. According to Matthew 4:3, the devil said to Jesus, "If you are the Son of God, command *these stones* to become *loaves of bread*." According to Luke 4:3, the devil said to Jesus, "If you are the Son of God, command *this stone* to become *bread*." Did the devil say "*these stones*" or "*this stone*"? Did the devil say "*bread*" or "*loaves of bread*"?

71. *A Question Concerning a Jesus Quotation*

While discussing a father's gifts to a son, did Jesus say, "If you then, who are evil, know how to give good gifts to your children, how much more will the heavenly Father give the *Holy Spirit* to those who ask him" (as reported in Luke 11:13), or did Jesus say, "If you then, who are evil, know how to give good gifts to your children, how much more will your Father in heaven give *good things* to those who ask him" (as reported in Matthew 7:11)? In other words, did Jesus use the phrase "*Holy Spirit*" or "*good things*"?

72. *A Question Concerning the Healing of the Centurion's Servant*

The gospels of Matthew and Luke contain accounts of Jesus healing at Capernaum the centurion's servant. Did the Roman officer *personally request* Jesus to heal his servant (as Matthew 8:5-13 reports), or did he make this request *through a delegation of Jewish elders* who went to Jesus and asked him to heal the servant (as Luke 7:1-10 reports)?

73. *A Question Concerning Protesters*

People protested to Jesus because his disciples did not fast. In response to this criticism Jesus remarked about the conduct of wedding guests, about putting unshrunk cloths on old garments, and about putting new wine in old wineskins (these remarks are recorded in Matthew 9:14-17, Mark 2:18-22, Luke 5:29-39). Did the *disciples of John* (as reported in Matthew 9:14) or did the *people* (as reported in Mark 2:18) or did the *Pharisees and their scribes* (as reported in Luke 5:30) bring to Jesus the complaint about his disciples' neglect of fasting?

74. *A Question Concerning Sandals*

When sending out his disciples did Jesus instruct them *to wear sandals* (as reported in Mark 6:9), or did he instruct them *not to wear sandals* (as reported in Matthew 10:10)?

75. *A Question Concerning a Staff*

While sending out disciples did Jesus instruct them to *carry a staff* (as

Mark 6:8 reports), or did he instruct them *not to carry a staff* (as Matthew 10:9-10 reports)?

76. *A Question Concerning a Request*
The request was made of Jesus that James and John be allowed to sit one on his right side and the other on his left side. Was this request made *by James and John* (as reported in Mark 10:35-37) or *by their mother* (as reported in Matthew 20:20-21)?

77. *A Question Concerning Elijah and John the Baptist*
Both Matthew 11:14 and Matthew 17:9-13 contain words of Jesus in which John the Baptist is described as being Elijah redivivus. Yet John the Baptist (in a statement recorded in John 1:21) denied that he was Elijah redivivus. Did Elijah *reappear* in John the Baptist (as Matthew 11:14 and Matthew 17:9-13 teach), or did he *not reappear* in John the Baptist (as John 1:21 asserts)?

78. *A Question Concerning Wisdom's Justification*
After observing that the Son of Man had been accused of being a glutton and a winebibber, did Jesus remark, "Wisdom is *justified by her works*" (as quoted in Matthew 11:19), or did Jesus remark, "Wisdom is justified *by all her children*" (as quoted in Luke 7:35)?

79. *A Question Concerning Being For and Against*
Did Jesus say "Anyone who is not for me is really against me" (Matthew 12:30), or did he say "Whoever is not against us is for us" (Mark 9:40)?

80. *A Question About Herod Antipas' Title*
Matthew 14:1-2, Mark 6:14-16, and Luke 9:7-9 contain accounts of Herod Antipas expressing the view that Jesus was John the Baptist raised from the dead. In Matthew 14:1 and in Luke 9:7 Herod Antipas is described as being a *tetrarch* (ruler of a fourth part). In Mark 6:14 he is described as being a *king*. Was Herod Antipas a *king* or a *tetrarch*?

81. *A Question Concerning the Hemorrhage Healing*
Jesus healed a woman who had suffered from a hemorrhage for twelve years. Was the woman with the hemorrhage healed *before* Jesus spoke to her (as Mark 5:28-29 and Luke 8:43-44 report), or was she healed *after* Jesus spoke to her (as Matthew 9:21-22 reports)?

82. *A Question Concerning a Sign for That Generation*
Responding to Pharisees who asked him for a sign, did Jesus say *no sign* would be given that generation (as Mark 8:12 affirms), or did he say that generation would be given *the sign of Jonah* (as Matthew 16:4 affirms)?

83. *A Question Concerning Divorce*
Assuming the Bible is inerrant, why did Jesus think that Deuteronomy 24:1 needed to be corrected and superceded by Genesis 1:27 and 2:24 (as reported in Matthew 19:3-9)?

84. *A Question Concerning a Jericho Healing*
While making his final trip to Jerusalem, did Jesus heal *one blind man* while passing through Jericho (as Mark 10:46-52 informs us), or did he heal *two blind men* while passing through Jericho (as Matthew 20:29-34 informs us)?

85. *A Question Concerning the Temple Cleansing*
Did the cleansing of the Temple occur *at the beginning* of Jesus' ministry (as John 2:13-17 reports), or did the Temple cleansing occur *at the end* of Jesus' ministry (as Matthew 21:12-13, Mark 11:15-17, and Luke 19:45-46 report)?

86. *A Question About the Hill Being Thrown Into the Sea*
Did Jesus utter the remark about the hill being thrown into the sea *one day* (Matthew 21:18-22) or *two days* (Mark 11:20-25) after his Triumphant Entry?

87. *A Question Concerning Zechariah's Father*

Was Zechariah, the martyr, the son of a man named *Barachiah* (as observed in Matthew 23:35), or was he the son of a man named *Jehoida* (as observed in II Chronicles 24:20-22)?

88. *A Question Concerning a Bed or a Field*

Matthew 24 and Luke 17 contain Jesus' descriptions of events which will take place when the Son of Man returns. In the course of these remarks, did Jesus say, "Then two men will be *in the field*; one is taken and one is left" (Matthew 24:40), or did he say, "I tell you, in that night there will be two men *in one bed*; one will be taken and the other left" (Luke 17:34)?

89. *A Question Concerning the Bethany Anointer*

Was the Bethany anointing performed by an *unnamed woman off the streets* (as reported in Matthew 26:6-13) or by *Mary*, Lazarus' sister (as reported in John 12:1-7)?

90. *Questions Concerning the Bethany Anointing*

Did Jesus' Bethany anointing take place *in the home of Simon the Leper* (as reported in Matthew 26:6-13) or in *Lazarus' house* (as reported in John 12:1-7)? Was the protest made by the *disciples* (Matthew 26:8) or by *Judas Iscariot* (John 12:4)?

91. *A Question Concerning the Head and Feet*

Did the Bethany anointing involve Jesus' *head* (as related in Matthew 26:6-13) or his *feet* (as related in John 12:1-7)?

92. *A Question Concerning the Akeldama Purchase*

The betrayal money paid to Judas Iscariot was used to purchase a field named *Akeldama* ("Field of Blood"). Matthew 27:3-8 makes it clear that the Field of Blood was purchased *after* Judas' death. Contrarily, Acts 1:18-19 makes it clear the Field of Blood was purchased *before* Judas' death. Did Judas' death *precede* or *follow* the purchase of the Field of Blood?

93. *A Question Concerning Judas' Death*

Did Judas *commit suicide by hanging himself* (as Matthew 27:3-5 relates), or did Judas *die from a puzzling sickness* which involved a *swelling of his body* (as Acts 1:18 relates)?

94. *A Question Concerning the Field Purchasers*

Was the "Field of Blood" *purchased by Judas* (as Acts 1:18-19 asserts), or was the "Field of Blood" *purchased by the Temple priests* (as Matthew 27:6-8 asserts)?

95. *A Question Concerning Thirty Pieces of Silver*

Did Judas take the thirty silver pieces of betrayal money *back to the chief priest and throw them down in the Temple* (as Matthew 27:3-5 recounts), or did Judas *take the thirty silver pieces of betrayal money and purchase a field* (as Acts 1:18 recounts)?

96. *A Question Concerning a Jeremiah Quotation*

Why does Matthew 27:9-10 attribute to Jeremiah a statement which does not appear in Jeremiah but is instead a loose quotation of Zechariah 11:12-13?

97. *A Question Concerning Jesus' Last Words*

Were Jesus' last words on the cross, "My God, my God, why hast thou forsaken me?" (Matthew 27:46) or "Father, into thy hands I commit my spirit!" (Luke 23:46) or "It is finished" (John 19:30)?

98. *A Question Concerning the Easter Resurrection Announcement*

Did a *young man in a white robe* (as reported in Mark 16:5) or did *an angel* (as reported in Matthew 28:2) or did *two men in dazzling apparel* (as reported in Luke 24:4) announce to the women at the tomb on Easter morning the news of Jesus' resurrection?

99. *A Question Concerning the Stone*

When the women arrived at the tomb on Easter morning, was the stone *already rolled back* (Mark 16:4, Luke 24:2, John 20:1) or did an earthquake and an angel of the Lord cause the stone to roll away *after the women arrived* (Matthew 28:1-2)?

100. *A Question Concerning Jesus' Final Appearance*
Did the risen Lord's final appearance to his disciples take place *in northern Palestine on a Galilean mountain* (Matthew 28:16-20), or did it take place *in southern Palestine at Bethany on Jerusalem's outskirts* (Luke 24:50-53)?

101. *A Question Concerning a Malachi Quotation*
Why does Mark 1:2 ascribe *to Isaiah* a statement ("God said, 'I will send my messenger ahead of you to prepare the way for you.'") which actually is a quotation *of Malachi 3:1*?

102. *A Question About Abiathar and Ahimelech*
Why does Mark 2:26 assert *Abiathar* was high priest during an episode in David's life which actually took place when *Ahimelech* was high priest (I Samuel 21:1-6)?

103. *A Question Concerning the Mustard Seed*
Why do the gospels observe in Mark 4:31 and Matthew 13:32 that the mustard seed is the smallest seed known to man when in reality many other seeds—such as the orchid—are smaller?

104. *A Question Concerning the Gerasene Demoniac*
When Jesus visited the land of the Gerasenes, did he heal *one* (Mark 5:2, Luke 8:27) or did he heal *two* (Matthew 8:28) demoniacs?

105. *A Question Concerning the Healed Man's Proclamation*
Did the healed Gerasene demoniac proclaim what Jesus had done for him in *one* city (as reported in Luke 8:39), or did he proclaim what Jesus had done for him in the *ten* cities known as the Decapolis (as reported in Mark 5:19-20)?

106. *A Question Concerning Bartimaeus*
Was Bartimaeus, blind beggar, healed while Jesus was *leaving* Jericho (as Mark 10:46 reports), or was Bartimaeus healed while Jesus was *approaching* Jericho (as Luke 18:35 reports)?

107. *A Question Concerning One Donkey or Two Donkeys*
In light of the assertions in Mark 11:7, Luke 19:35, and John 12:14 that Jesus rode *one* donkey into Jerusalem during his triumphant entry, why does Matthew 21:1-7 curiously assert that Jesus rode *two* donkeys into Jerusalem during the triumphant entry?

108. *A Question Concerning When to Flee*
While warning his disciples about the Temple's destruction, did Jesus say, *"But when you see the desolating sacrilege set up where it ought not to be*—let the reader understand—then let those who are in Judea flee to the mountains"* (Mark 13:14), or did he say, *"But when you see Jerusalem surrounded by armies,* then know that its desolation has come near. Then let those who are in Judea flee to the mountains"* (Luke 21:20-21)?

109. *A Question Concerning Jesus' Final Meal*
Was Jesus' final meal with his disciples a *Passover meal* (as Mark 14:12 makes clear), or was it a meal eaten prior *to Passover* (as John 18:28 and 19:14 make clear)?

110. *A Question Concerning Cock Crowing*
Did Jesus say to Peter, "Truly, I say to you, this very night, *before the cock crows,* you will deny me three times" (Matthew 26:34), or did Jesus say to Peter, "Truly I say to you, this very night, *before the cock crows twice,* you will deny me three times." (Mark 14:30)?

111. *A Question Concerning When the Cock Crowed*
Did Peter deny Jesus *while a cock was crowing* (Luke 22:34,60), or *did the cock crow after* Peter denied Jesus (Matthew 26:34, 74-75), or did Peter deny Jesus *before the cock crowed a second time* (Mark 14:30,72)?

112. *A Question Concerning the Time of the Crucifixion*
Was Jesus crucified *at nine o'clock in the morning* (Mark 15:25) or *after the noon hour* (John 19:14)?

113. *A Question Concerning the Empty Tomb's Discovery*
On Easter morning did *one woman* (John 20:1) or did *three women* (Mark 16:1) discover Jesus' empty tomb?

114. *A Question Concerning When the Tomb Visit Occurred*
On Easter morning did the visit to the empty tomb occur *at sunrise* (as Mark 16:2 states), or did the visit occur *while it was still dark* (as John 20:1 states)?

115. *A Question Concerning Mary Magdalene's Conduct*
On Easter morning did Mary Magdalene *report the empty tomb to Peter* (as reported in John 20:2), or did she *say nothing to anyone* (as reported in Mark 16:8)?

116. *A Question Concerning the Wilderness Perishing*
Did *twenty-three thousand* (as stated in I Corinthians 10:8) or did *twenty-four thousand* (as stated in Numbers 25:1-9) Israelites perish in the wilderness because of idolatry and sexual immorality?

117. *A Question Concerning the Premise of Hebrews 9:22*
In view of the assertion of Hebrews 9:22 that "without the shedding of blood there is no forgiveness of sins," why did the Mosaic law provide for a sin offering consisting of *flour* rather than blood (as stated in Leviticus 5:11-13)?

118. *A Question Concerning Plant Life*
Photosynthesis (the formation of carbohydrates in the chlorophyll-containing tissues of plants by exposure to sunlight) is a necessary process for vegetation to exist. According to the first Genesis creation account, plant life was created (Genesis 1:11-13) before the sun was

created (Genesis 1:14-18). How was it possible for vegetation to exist on earth prior to the sun's existence?

119. *Questions Concerning the Reconciling of the Two Genesis Creation Accounts.*

Genesis contains two different accounts of the world's creation. The first account is found in Genesis 1:1-2:4; the second is found in Genesis 2:5-24. These diverse accounts employ different names for God; the first account uses for God the Hebrew word *Elohim* whereas the second uses for God the Hebrew name *Yahweh*. The second account is vividly anthropomorphic in its conception of God while the first one is not. The *order of creation* found in these two accounts differs. These differences become obvious when the two accounts are compared.

The Seven-day Account of Creation in Genesis 1:1-2:4	*The Yahweh Account of Creation in Genesis 2:5-24*
1. On day one light was created in the midst of a primeval, turbulent sea (1:1-3).	1. Creation began with a primeval desert which was void of rain. This desert was periodically moistened with subterranean water (2:5-6).
2. On day two the vault of heaven was created (1:6-8).	2. Man was created out of dirt (2:7).
3. On day three dry land, trees, and vegetation were created (1:9-13).	3. The Garden of Eden was planted (2:8) by Yahweh.
4. On day four the stars, sun, and moon were created (1:14-18).	4. Trees—including the tree of life and the tree of the knowledge of good and evil—were created (2:9).

5. On day five living creatures in the air and sea (fish, birds, sea-monsters) were created (1:20-23).

5. Cattle, wild animals, and birds were created out of dirt (2:19-20).

6. On day six living creatures on earth (cattle, reptiles, wild animals, and man—male and female) were created (1:24-31).

6. Woman was created out of the man's rib (2:21-22).

7. On day seven God completed the work he had been doing and ceased from all his work (2:1-4).

Questions arise. Was the world created out of a *primeval watery chaos* (1:1-3), or was it created out of a *primeval desert* (2:5-6)? Was man created *toward the end* of the creation process (1:24-31), or was he created *at the beginning* of the creation process (2:17)? Was the world created by *Elohim* or by *Yahweh*? Which creation order is correct—the creation order found in Genesis 1:1-2:4 or the creation order found in Genesis 2:5-24? Why is no reference to the Garden of Eden found in the first creation account? Was the world created twice?

120. *A Question Concerning the Morality of Slavery*
The Bible takes human slavery for granted. Nowhere in biblical literature is slavery explicitly condemned. Instead, the Bible contains passages like Leviticus 25:45-46 which asserts:

> As for your male and female slaves whom you may have: you may buy male and female slaves from among the nations that are round about you. You may also buy from among strangers who sojourn with you and their families that are with you, who have been born on your land; and they may be your property. You may bequeath them to your sons after you, to inherit as a possession forever.

In Exodus 21:20-21 a slave is recognized as being his master's *property*. This passage reads:

> If a man takes a stick and beats his slave, whether male or female, and the slave dies on the spot, the man is to be punished. But if the slave does not die for a day or two, the master is not to be punished. The loss of his property is punishment enough.

The Law of Moses contains detailed slave legislation dealing with such matters as drilling a hole through a slave's ear (Exodus 21:6), selling a daughter into slavery (Exodus 21:7), beating a slave with a stick (Exodus 21:26-27). Ephesians spells out guidelines for proper slave behavior (Ephesians 6:5-8). The letter to Philemon concerns Onesimus, a runaway slave sent back to his owner by St. Paul. In fact, the Bible carries the institution of slavery all the way back to Noah (Genesis 9:25-27). Is the Bible's approval of human slavery morally acceptable?

121. *A Question Concerning the Morality of Spitting on a Daughter*
Numbers 12:13-14 teaches that a daughter remains in disgrace for seven days after her father spits in her face. Is spitting in a daughter's face a morally-acceptable paternal practice?

122. *A Question Concerning the Credibility of the Earth Splitting Open*
Is it possible for the ground to split open, thereby permitting people living on this earth to fall headlong into the realm of the dead (as recounted in Numbers 16:31-34)?

123. *A Question Concerning the Morality of Murdering War Prisoners*
Deuteronomy 20:13 provides for the annihilation of war prisoners. Is the slaughtering of war captives a practice which is morally acceptable?

124. *A Question Concerning the Morality of Marrying a Raper*
Should an unengaged woman marry a man who rapes her—provided her father has been paid fifty pieces of silver (as Deuteronomy 22:28-29 commands)?

125. *A Question Concerning People Born Out of Wedlock*
Should people born out of wedlock and their descendants be excluded from God's people (as proscribed in Deuteronomy 23:2)?

126. *A Question Concerning the Morality of Hand Amputation*
Deuteronomy 25:11-12 states, "If two men are having a fight and the wife of one tries to help her husband by grabbing hold of the other man's genitals, show her no mercy. Cut off her hand." Is hand amputation a morally-acceptable practice?

127. *Questions Concerning the Credibility of Biblical Cosmology*
Does the sun move around the earth (Joshua 10:12-14); is the earth motionless (Psalm 93:1); do rooms exist in the sky for storing hail and snow (Job 38:22); is the sea restrained by bolted gates (Job 38:10); does the sky have windows (Malachi 3:10); is the earth supported underneath with pillars (Job 9:6, 38:6); is the sky as hard as metal (Job 37:18); does the earth have four corners (Revelation 7:1)?

128. *A Question Concerning the Morality of Horse Crippling*
Joshua 11 contains an account of a battle at the waters of Merom between the Jews and their Canaanite enemies. With reference to these enemies (according to Joshua 11:6) the Lord said to Joshua, "Do not be afraid of them, for at this time tomorrow I shall deliver them to Israel all dead men; you shall hamstring their horses and burn their chariots." Joshua 11:9 reports that the Jews carried out God's command to hamstring (i.e., to cripple by cutting leg tendons) the horses of the Canaanites. Is cruelty to animals morally-acceptable behavior?

129. *A Question Concerning the Morality of Genocide*
The Old Testament book of Joshua is a war document. It contains an account of the Jewish conquest of Canaan ("the promised land") in the 1200s B.C. This war document informs us that God ordered the mass extermination of the Canaanites. For example, Joshua 11:19-20 asserts:

Except for the Hivites who lived in Gibeon, not one of their cities came to terms with the Israelites; all were taken by storm. It was the LORD'S purpose that they should offer an obstinate resistance to the Israelites in battle, and that thus they should be annihilated without mercy and utterly destroyed, as the LORD had commanded Moses.

Can moral approval be given to the commanding of a pogrom against the Canaanites? Can Jews or Christians take pride in the fact that the book of Joshua contains one of history's earliest known accounts of a human holocaust? To express the issue another way, does God approve of genocide?

130. *A Question Concerning the Morality of Slaughtering Forty-two Children*
II Kings 2:23-24 reports that forty-two children were mauled by bears as punishment for having called Elisha a bald head. Is bear mauling of children a morally-approvable action?

131. *A Question Concerning the Credibility of Different Burial Places for the Same Corpse*
I Samuel 31:13 reports that Saul's corpse was buried at Jabesh under a *tamarisk tree*. Contrarily, I Chronicles 10:12 reports that it was buried at Jabesh under an *oak*. How was it possible for the *same corpse* to be buried at Jabesh under *two different trees?*

132. *A Question Concerning the Morality of Dashing Children Against Rocks*
Psalm 137:9 applauds the physical bashing of children. Is child battering against rocks a morally-acceptable procedure?

133. *A Question Concerning Geography*
How is it physically or geographically possible to pass through the territory of the Decapolis while traveling from Sidon to the Sea of Galilee (as reported in Mark 7:31)?

134. *A Question Concerning the Total Absence of Parables in the Fourth Gospel*

In the first three gospels (Matthew, Mark, and Luke) Jesus is portrayed as a parable teller. His parables—like the one concerning the prodigal son or the one concerning the good Samaritan—are familiar to New Testament readers. Mark 4:34 asserts that Jesus *did not speak to his disciples except in parables.*

In John's gospel, however, Jesus is presented as a teacher who *did not tell parables.* Indeed, a total absence of parables is a puzzling feature of the Fourth Gospel.

Questions emerge. Did Jesus *tell parables* (as Matthew, Mark, and Luke make clear), or did he *not tell parables* (as John's gospel suggests)? If it be true that Jesus did not speak to his disciples *except in parables* (as Mark 4:34 observes), why do *no parables* appear in Jesus' lengthy discourses (to his disciples) which are recorded in the Fourth Gospel? In other words, are the Jesus discourses in the Fourth Gospel historically accurate?

135. *A Question Concerning Seeing God*

Isaiah 6:1 states that Isaiah saw the Lord seated on a throne, high and exalted. Acts 7:54-56 reports that Stephen *gazed into heaven* and saw the Son of Man standing at *God's right hand.* Exodus 24:9-12 observes that Moses, Aaron, Nadab, Abihu, and seventy of the elders of Israel *saw the God of Israel.* In this Exodus passage explicit reference is made to *God's feet* and to his *hand.* Exodus 33:18-23 reports that Moses was to be allowed to see God's back but not God's face.

John 1:18, however, states: "No man has ever seen God at any time."

Which tradition is true—the tradition that *no man has ever seen God* or the tradition that Moses, Aaron, Nadab, Abihu, seventy elders, Isaiah, and Stephen *saw* God?

136. *Questions Concerning the Priestly Cities*

According to Joshua 21:1-42 and I Chronicles 6:54-81, the priests and Levites were granted certain cities (with their surrounding pastures) in which to live in Palestine. Below is a listing of these priestly cities as they are recorded in Joshua and I Chronicles.

An Alphabetical Listing of Priestly Cities Cited in Joshua 21:1-42	*An Alphabetical Listing of Priestly Cities Cited in I Chronicles 6:54-81*
Abdon	Abdon
Aijalon	Aijalon
Ain	
Almon	
	Alemeth
	Anem
	Aner
	Ashan
Anathoth	Anathoth
Ashtaroth	
Beeshterah	
Bezer	Bezer
Bethhoron	Bethhoron
Bethshemesh	Bethshemesh
Bileam	
Daberath	Daberath
Debir	Debir
Dimnah	
Elteke	
Engannim	
Eshtemoa	Eshtemoa
Gathrimmon	Gathrimmon
Geba	Geba
Gezer	Gezer
Gibbethon	

Gibeon	
Golan	Golan
Hammon	
Hammothdor	
Hebron	Hebron
Helkath	
Heshbon	Heshbon
Holon	Hilen
Hukok	
Jahaz	
Jarmuth	
Jattir	Jattir
Jahzah	
Jazer	Jazer
Jokneam	Jokmeam
Juttah	
Kartah	
	Kartan
Kedemoth	Kedemoth
Kedesh	Kedesh
Kiriatharba	
Kishion	
Libnah	Libnah
Mahanaim	Mahanaim
Mephaath	Mephaath
Mishal	Mashal
Nahalal	
Ramoth	Ramoth
Rehob	Rehob
Rimmono	
Shechem	Shechem
Tabor	
Tanach	Tanach

A comparison of these two columns reveals that the Chronicles list mentions *twelve cities not mentioned in Joshua*. Comparison also indicates that the Joshua list mentions *twenty cities not mentioned in Chronicles*. Why do these lists not agree? Moreover, the Joshua list contains *forty-eight* city names while the Chronicles list contains *forty* city names. Why this *numerical* discrepancy?

137. *Questions Concerning the Moving of the Ark of the Covenant*

II Samuel 6 and I Chronicles 13 contain parallel accounts of King David moving the ark of the covenant to Jerusalem. The ark of the covenant was conveyed on a cart pulled by oxen. The oxen stumbled while pulling this cart. II Samuel 6:6 states that they stumbled at the *threshing floor of Nacon*. But I Chronicles 13:9 states that they stumbled at the *threshing floor of Chidon*. Which of these traditions is correct? Moreover, II Samuel 6:2 states that King David retrieved the ark of the covenant from a town named *Baalejudah*. But I Chronicles 13:5 observes that King David retrieved the ark from a town named *Kiriathjearim*. Which tradition is correct—*Baalejudah* or *Kiriathjearim*?

138. *A Question Concerning Kish*

Kish was the father of Saul, the first Jewish king. Was Kish the son of a man named *Abiel* (as noted in I Samuel 9:1), or was he the son of a man named *Ner* (as noted in I Chronicles 8:33)?

139. *A Question Concerning Basemath*

Basemath was one of Esau's wives. Was she the daughter of *Elon* the *Hittite* (as noted in Genesis 26:34), or was she the daughter of *Ishmael* (as noted in Genesis 36:3)?

140. *A Question Concerning Samuel's Ancestry*

From which of Jacob's sons did Samuel, the seer, descend? Was Samuel a descendant of *Ephraim* (as reported in I Samuel 1:1), or was he a descendant of *Levi* (as reported in I Chronicles 6:28)?

141. *A Question Concerning the Naming of the Field of Blood*
Matthew 27:3-10 contains an account of Judas' reaction to having betrayed Jesus. This Matthean account states that the Jewish priests viewed the thirty pieces of silver which Judas returned as "blood money" (money paid to secure Jesus' betrayal and death). Subsequently, the priests purchased a field with Judas' betrayal money and named it "Field of Blood" *because it had been purchased with blood money.*

Acts 1:18-19 contains a different reason for the field being called "Field of Blood." According to Acts, the field was so named because it became *blood-covered* as a result of the bizarre, explosive disintegration of Judas' body. ("Judas fell forward on the ground, and burst open, so that his entrails poured out. This became known to everyone in Jerusalem, and they named the property in their own language Akeldama, which means 'field of blood'").

Why was the "Field of Blood" so named? Was it so named because it was purchased with *blood money,* or was it so named because it became *blood-covered* as a result of Judas' grotesque death?

142. *Questions Concerning Ahimelech*
I Samuel 22:9 and 11 state that Ahimelech, the priest, was the son of Ahitub. This father-son relationship is expressed again in I Samuel 22:20—a verse which also observes that Ahimelech in turn was *the father* of Abiathar. Contrarily—however—II Samuel 8:17 states that Ahimelech was *the son* (rather than the father) of Abiathar. Was Ahimelech *the father of Abiathar* (as I Samuel 22:9-11 reports) or was he *the son of Abiathar* (as II Samuel 8:17 reports)? Moreover, was Ahimelech *the son of Abiathar* (as II Samuel 8:17 indicates), or was he *the son of Ahitub* (as I Samuel 22:9 and 11 indicate)?

143. *A Question Concerning the Title on Jesus' Cross*
The Romans nailed to Jesus' cross a title (sign) which spelled out the

charge on which Jesus was crucified. Did the title read "This is Jesus the King of the Jews" (Matthew 27:37) or "The King of the Jews" (Mark 15:26) or "This is the King of the Jews" (Luke 23:38) or "Jesus of Nazareth, the King of the Jews" (John 19:19)?

144. *A Question Concerning the Lord's Prayer*

Jesus taught the Lord's prayer as a model petition. In Matthew's gospel he articulated the Lord's prayer while delivering the Sermon on the Mount (Matthew 6:7-13) and while speaking *to a multitude* (Matthew 5:1). In Luke's gospel, however, Jesus taught the Lord's prayer *to his disciples while* "praying in a certain place" (Luke 11:1-4). Did Jesus teach the Lord's prayer *to a multitude* or *to his disciples* (Luke 11:2)? Was it a part of the Sermon on the Mount (Matthew 6:7-13) or was it not a part of the Sermon on the Mount (Luke 11:1-4)?

145. *A Question Concerning Sabbath Rest*

The ten commandments are listed in Exodus 20 and in Deuteronomy 5. The fourth commandment concerns Sabbath rest and lists those who are to rest on the Sabbath. The lists are as follows:

Those Who Are to Rest According to Exodus 20:8-11	*Those Who Are to Rest According to Deuteronomy 5:12-15*
you	you
son	son
daughter	daughter
man servant	man servant
maid servant	maid servant
	ox
	ass
cattle	cattle
sojourner	sojourner

The *ox* and *ass* are mentioned in Deuteronomy but not in Exodus. Did God *exclude* or *include* the ox and ass in Sabbath rest?

146. *A Question Concerning the High Priest at Jesus' Trial*
John 18:13 observes that Caiaphas was *high priest* and father-in-law of
Annas. John 18:13 also states that Jesus was led before Annas for
examination. In the course of the examination before Annas "one of
the officers standing by struck Jesus with his hand, saying, 'Is that how
you answer the high priest?'" This quotation makes it clear that Annas
(not Caiaphas) was high priest. That Annas was the high priest is
confirmed by John 18:19 which states in regard to Annas, "The high
priest then questioned Jesus about his disciples and his teaching." Yet
John 18:24—puzzlingly—states that Annas sent Jesus bound to
Caiaphas the high priest. Who was high priest at the time of Jesus'
arrest? Was it *Annas* (as stated in John 18:19 and 22) or *Caiaphas* (as
stated in John 18:13 and 24)?

147. *A Question Concerning Moses*
The second chapter of Exodus tells of Moses murdering an Egyptian.
In the aftermath of this murder, Exodus 2:14-15 reports, Moses
became *frightened* and fled Egypt. Moreover, the text asserts, "When
Pharaoh heard of the matter he would have killed Moses, but Moses
fled from Pharaoh" (Exodus 2:15).

Hebrews 11:27, contrarily, asserts concerning Moses, "It was by faith
that he left Egypt and was *not afraid* of the king's anger."

When Moses left Egypt, *was he frightened* (as Exodus reports), or was
he not afraid (as Hebrews reports)?

148. *A Question Concerning Benejaakan*
Numbers 33:5-40 contains an account of Jewish wilderness wanderings immediately before Aaron's death (Numbers 33:38). This account states that the Jews encamped at a place named *Moserah* and
then moved on to a place named *Benejaakan* (Numbers 33:31).

Deuteronomy 10:6-9 also contains an account of Jewish wilderness
wanderings immediately prior to Aaron's death (Deuteronomy 10:6).

This account, contrarily, states that the Jews encamped at *Benejaakan* and then moved to *Moserah*.

Thus the question arises: Did the Jews (immediately prior to Aaron's death) march *from Moserah to Benejaakan*, or did they march in the opposite direction, i.e., *from Benejaakan to Moserah*? Which direction is correct?

149. *A Question Concerning the Feast of Tabernacles*
Did the Feast of Tabernacles have a duration of *seven days* (as stated in Deuteronomy 16:15), or did it have a duration of *eight days* (as stated in Leviticus 23:36)?

150. *A Question Concerning Isaac's Final Illness*
Genesis 25:26 states that Isaac was *sixty years old* when Esau (Isaac's son) was born. Genesis 26:34 states that Esau was *forty years old* when he married. Thus Isaac would have been *one hundred years old* at the time of Esau's marriage. Isaac—at the age of one hundred—perceived he was near death (as reported in Genesis 27:1-4). Genesis 35:28, however, observes that Isaac did not die until he was one hundred and eighty years old. Did Isaac spend *eighty years* on his death bed (as Genesis 27:1-4 and Genesis 35:28 suggest)?

151. *A Question Concerning Nebuchanezzar*
Jehoiakim was king of Judah, and Nebuchanezzar was king of Babylon. Daniel 1:1 states that in the *third year* of Jehoiakim's reign, Nebuchanezzar came to Jerusalem and beseiged it. But Jeremiah 25:1 reports that Nebuchanezzar did not become king of Babylon until the *fourth year* of Jehoiakim's reign. How could Nebuchanezzar—king of Babylon—have beseiged Jerusalem in Jehoiakim's *third year* since he did not become king of Babylon until Jehoiakim's *fourth year*? If Nebuchanezzar beseiged Jerusalem during Jehoiakim's reign (as Daniel 1:1 states), why does II Kings 24:10-15 report a contrary tradition that Nebuchanezzar did not beseige Jerusalem until *after* Jehoiakim's death?

152. *A Question Concerning Noah*

Genesis 6:19-21 states that Noah was commanded to take a *single pair* of every species into the ark; Genesis 6:22 asserts that Noah obeyed this command. But Genesis 7:2-3 states that Noah was commanded to take *seven pairs* of clean animals and a *single pair* of unclean animals into the ark; Genesis 7:5 asserts that Noah obeyed this command. Which of these contradictory traditions is correct? If it be true that Noah took into the ark *seven pairs* of clean animals and a *single pair* of unclean animals (as reported in Genesis 7:2-5), why does Genesis 7:8-9 state that only a *single pair* (male and female) of animals entered the ark with Noah?

153. *A Question Concerning Evil*

I Samuel 16 tells of Saul's and David's relationship. This account states that an evil spirit periodically went forth from God (I Samuel 16:15 and 23) and tormented Saul. Is God the ground or source of evil? As Amos 3:6 suggests, is God the one who brings evil upon cities?

154. *A Question Concerning the Ten Commandments*

Exodus 34:27-28 states that *Moses* wrote the ten commandments on tablets of stone. Contrarily, Deuteronomy 10:1-4 states that *God* wrote the ten commandments on stone tablets. Who wrote the ten commandments? Did God write them, or did Moses write them?

155. *A Question Concerning the Sun*

People today believe the earth revolves around the sun. In the ancient world, however, most people believed the sun revolved around the earth. This view is reflected in the Bible. Joshua 10, for example, contains an account of a battle between the Jews and the Amorites. This account reports that on the day of battle the sun stood still in the sky and "did not hasten to go down for about a whole day" (Joshua 10:13). II Kings 20:8-11 and Isaiah 38:8 report that the sun (in Hezekiah's time) reversed its course and caused a shadow on the dial of Ahaz to move backward. Does the sun—contrary to modern belief—revolve around the earth?

156. *A Question Concerning Concurrent Ministries*
According to John 3:22-24, Jesus began his ministry and baptized in Judea *before* John the Baptist was put in prison. Matthew 4:12 and Mark 1:14, contrarily, state that Jesus began his ministry *after* John's imprisonment. Did Jesus and John have concurrent ministries (as John 3:22-24 states), or did they not have concurrent ministries (as Matthew 4:12 and Mark 1:14 suggest)?

157. *A Question Concerning Jesus' Baptism*
Matthew 3:13-15 and Mark 1:9 report that Jesus was baptized by John the Baptist. Luke 3:18-21, however, recounts that Jesus was not baptized until *after* John had been imprisoned (thus making it impossible for John to have baptized Jesus). The gospel of John has *no account* of Jesus being baptized (John 1:29-42). Was Jesus baptized *before* or *after* John's imprisonment? Was Jesus baptized *by John or by some unknown party*? Was Jesus not baptized (as John's gospel implies)?

158. *A Question Concerning Altar Steps*
Did God decree for altars *to have steps* (as commanded in Ezekiel 43:17), or did God decree for altars *not to have steps* (as mentioned in Exodus 20:26)?

159. *A Question Concerning Hobab*
Was Hobab, Moses' father-in-law, a *Midianite* (as stated in Numbers 10:29) or was he a *Kenite* (as reported in Judges 4:11)?

160. *A Question Concerning the Order of the Bread and Cup at the Last Supper*
The New Testament contains four accounts of the Last Supper. Three of these accounts (Matthew 26:26-29, Mark 14:22-25, I Corinthians 11:23-26) relate that Jesus served *bread* to the disciples and then served a *cup of wine*. Luke 22:14-23, however, contains a variant tradition. This Lucan account asserts that Jesus *first* served the *cup*

(Luke 22:17) and then served bread (Luke 22:19). Which sequence is correct? The *bread-cup* sequence in Matthew, Mark, and I Corinthians or the *cup-bread* (or *cup-bread-cup*) sequence in Luke?

161. A *Question Concerning a Soil Tiller*
Genesis 2:15 reports that God placed Adam in the Garden of Eden *to till* and to keep the garden. Moreover, Genesis 3:23 states that Adam *tilled soil* outside the Garden of Eden. Genesis 4:2 asserts that Cain (Adam's son) was also a *tiller* of the ground. In light of the fact that both Adam and Cain were soil tillers, why does Genesis 9:20 assert that Noah (who lived much later than Adam and Cain) was the *first person* who tilled soil? In other words, *who first tilled soil*, Adam and Cain (as Genesis 2:15, 3:23, and 4:2 state) or Noah (as Genesis 9:20 reports)? This question presupposes the Noah discussion found on pp. 554-56 of Vol. 3 of *The Interpreter's Dictionary of the Bible* (Nashville: Abingdon Press, 1962).

162. A *Question Concerning Sailing Away from Philippi*
Philippi is a hill-top city located miles inland; it is not a seaport. Thus how was it possible for Paul and his companions *to sail away from Philippi* (as Acts 20:6 reports they did)?

163. A *Question Concerning Female Behavior*
I Corinthians 14:34-35 asserts that women should not speak in church. Indeed, this text affirms that for a woman to speak in church is a "shameful" deed. Should women be prohibited from speaking publicly in services of Christian worship?

164. A *Question Concerning Jesus' Baptizing Practice*
John 3:22 states that Jesus baptized. John 4:2 states that Jesus did not baptize. Did Jesus baptize others (as reported in John 3:22) or did he *not* baptize (as reported in John 4:2)?

165. A *Question Concerning Dogs*
Revelation 22:15 asserts that dogs will be excluded from heaven. This

passage also classifies dogs with sorcerers, fornicators, murderers, idolaters, and everyone who loves and practices falsehood. Should dogs (man's best friend) be so categorized and be ostracized from heaven?

166. *A Question Concerning the Vanity of Life*
Ecclesiastes 1:2 and 12:8 assert, "Vanity of vanities. All is vanity." Is Ecclesiastes correct in affirming that human existence is an exercise in futility and vain pursuits? In other words, is life an empty bag?

167. *A Question Concerning Falling and Standing*
The account of Paul's Damascus Road experience in Acts 9:7 states that Paul's companions *stood*. The parallel account in Acts 26:14 states that they *fell to the ground*. Which of these contradictory accounts is correct?

168. *A Question Concerning the Heavenly Voice*
The account of Paul's Damascus Road experience in Acts 9:7 reports that Paul's companions *heard* the heavenly voice. The parallel account in Acts 22:9 states that Paul's companions *did not hear* the heavenly voice? Which of these contradictory accounts is correct?

169. *A Question Concerning a Prophet*
I Kings 20:35-36 reports that a prophet was killed by a lion as punishment for being unwilling to assault a fellow prophet. Is this episode morally edifying?

170. *A Question Concerning Benjamin's Birthplace*
Genesis 35:16-19 reports that Benjamin, one of Jacob's twelve sons, was born between Bethel and Ephrath (that is, Bethlehem). This statement means that Benjamin was born *in Israel*. But Genesis 35:24-26 reports that Benjamin was born in Paddam-aram (that is, *Syria*). Was Benjamin born in *Syria* or in *Israel*?

171. *A Question Concerning Sexual Intercourse*
Leviticus 15:18 asserts that when a man copulates with a woman and experiences an emission of semen, both become unclean until evening and both must bathe. Does a normal biological function like sexual intercourse make a man or a woman impure?

172. *A Question Concerning Menstruation*
Leviticus 15:19-24 asserts that a menstruous woman is unclean for seven days. Moreover, the passage teaches that everything a menstruous woman sits or lies upon becomes unclean (as does a person who touches a menstruous woman). Does a normal biological function like menstruation convey uncleanness?

173. *A Question Concerning Defecation*
Leviticus 15:1-12 states that defecation makes a person impure. The view is expressed that everything upon which a person who has defecated lies or sits (including saddles) becomes unclean. Does a normal biological function like defecating transmit uncleanness?

174. *A Question Concerning Fat*
Leviticus 3:17 forbids the eating of fat. Yet in Nehemiah 8:10, Deuteronomy 32:13-14, Isaiah 25:6, and Psalm 63:5 the eating of fat is commended. Does the Bible *approve* or *disapprove* eating fat?

175. *A Question Concerning Mankind's Life Span*
Genesis 6:3 states that man's life span is one hundred and twenty years. Assuming that man's life span is one hundred and twenty years, how was it possible for Arpachshad (Genesis 11:12-13), Shelah (Genesis 11:14-15) and Eber (Genesis 11:16-17) to live to be *over* four hundred years old? How was it possible for Peleg (Genesis 11:18-19) and Reu (Genesis 11:20-21) to live to be *over* two hundred years old?

176. *A Question Concerning Canaan*
Genesis 9:18 reports that Canaan was the son of Ham and was *Noah's*

grandson. Contrarily, Genesis 9:24-25 suggests that Canaan was *Noah's youngest son*. Was Canaan Noah's *youngest son* or was he *Noah's grandson*?

177. *A Question Concerning a Mountain*
Matthew 4:8 reports that the devil took Jesus to a high mountain and showed him all the kingdoms of the world and the glory of them. What mountain on earth is high enough to serve as a vantage point from which Jesus and the devil saw all the kingdoms of earth (particularly in view of the earth's sphericity)?

178. *A Question Concerning the Earth's People*
Genesis 9:19 reports that the whole earth was peopled from the sons of Noah (Shem, Ham, and Japheth). What historical, archaeological, or anthropological evidence suggests that the people of India, China, Japan, southeast Asia, Melanesia, Micronesia, Polynesia, and black, sub-Sahara Africa are descendants of Shem, Ham, and Japheth?

179. *A Question Concerning Ahab's Drought*
I Kings 17 and 18 recount a drought which occurred when Ahab was king and Elijah was a prophet. According to I Kings 18:1, this drought came to an end *during its third year*. Thus the drought's length was two years plus an indeterminate part of a third year. If it be true that Ahab's drought was *less than three years in length*, why do Luke 4:25 and James 5:17 contain the contrary tradition that Ahab's drought lasted for *three and a half years*?

180. *A Question Concerning Joram's Son*
Matthew 1:8 reports that Joram's son was a man named *Uzziah*. I Chronicles 3:11 and II Kings 8:24, contrarily, report that Joram's son was a man named *Ahaziah*. Furthermore, I Chronicles identifies *Uzziah* (also known as Azariah) as being Joram's great-great-great grandson. Was Joram's son named *Uzziah* or *Ahaziah*? Was Uzziah Joram's son or was he his *great-great-great-grandson*?

181. *A Question Concerning Jesus' Grandfather*

Luke 3:23 states that Jesus' grandfather was named *Heli*. But Matthew 1:16 states that Jesus' grandfather was named *Jacob*. Was Jesus' grandfather named *Jacob* or *Heli*?

182. *A Question Concerning Thirteen Generations*

Matthew 1:17 states there were *fourteen generations* from the deportation to Babylon until the Messiah's birth. *These fourteen generations* are listed in Matthew 1:12-16 as follows:

1. Jeconia	to	Shealtiel
2. Shealtiel	to	Zerubbabel
3. Zerubbabel	to	Abiud
4. Abiud	to	Eliakim
5. Eliakim	to	Azor
6. Azor	to	Zadok
7. Zadok	to	Achim
8. Achim	to	Eliud
9. Eliud	to	Eleazar
10. Eleazar	to	Matthan
11. Matthan	to	Jacob
12. Jacob	to	Joseph
13. Joseph	to	Jesus

A perusal of these names, however, reveals *thirteen* rather than *fourteen generations*. Why does the genealogy in Matthew 1:12-16 curiously list *thirteen generations* instead of *fourteen generations* as it claims?

183. *A Question Concerning Rahab the Harlot*

Rahab was a harlot who sheltered men dispatched by Joshua to spy out Jericho. She lived in the 1200s B.C., prior to the era of the Judges. Matthew 1:5, contrarily, locates her centuries later during the time of Salmon, a man who lived two generations before King David. Why does Matthew's genealogy anachronistically locate Rahab some *two centuries* later than when she actually lived?

184. *A Question Concerning Rachel's Tomb*

Genesis 35:19 and Genesis 48:7 locate Rachel's tomb in proximity to *Bethlehem* (which is in the *territory of Judah*). I Samuel 10:2, contrarily, locates Rachel's tomb at *Zelzah* in the *territory of Benjamin*. Which report is correct? Was Rachel's tomb located near Bethlehem in the territory of Judah or was it located at Zelzah in the territory of Benjamin?

185. *A Question Concerning Three Missing Names*

Matthew 1:6-8 contains a genealogy from David to Azariah. A similar genealogy is found in I Chronicles 3:9-11. These genealogies read as follows:

I Chronicles 3:9-11	*Matthew 1:6-8*
1. David	1. David
2. Solomon	2. Solomon
3. Rehoboam	3. Rehoboam
4. Abijah	4. Abijah
5. Asa	5. Asa
6. Jehoshaphat	6. Jehoshaphat
7. Joram	7. Joram
8. *Ahaziah*	
9. *Joash*	
10. *Amaziah*	
11. Azariah	8. Azariah

Matthew's genealogy excludes three names (or three generations) found in I Chronicles: *Ahaziah, Joash,* and *Amaziah.* Why this exclusion? Was *Ahaziah* (as I Chronicles reports) or *Azariah* (as Matthew reports) Joram's son?

186. *A Question Concerning Nazareth*

Matthew 2:23 observes that Jesus settled in a town named Nazareth in order to fulfill the words spoken by the *prophets,* "He shall be called a Nazarene" (i.e., a person from Nazareth). This statement suggests that *multiple references to Nazareth* appear in the Old Testament prophets. A reading of the Old Testament prophets, however, reveals they do not refer a single time to Nazareth. Indeed, no reference to Nazareth can be found anywhere in the Old Testament or in the Talmud or in Josephus. Why does Matthew 2:23 state that the *prophets* refer to Nazareth (or a Nazarene) when in reality they do not?

187. *A Question Concerning Amminadab*
Amminadab was one of Jesus' ancestors. He is mentioned both in Luke's and in Matthew's genealogy. Luke 3:33 states that Amminadab's father was a man named *Admin*. But Matthew 1:4 states that Amminadab's father was a man named Ram. Was Amminadab's father named *Admin* (as noted in Luke 3:33) or was he named *Ram* (as noted in Matthew 1:4)?

188. *A Question Concerning The Sandal Observation of John the Baptist*
Matthew 3:11, Mark 1:7, and John 1:27 contain the sandal observation of John the Baptist.

Matthew 3:11 reads, "He who is coming after me is mightier than I, whose sandals I am not worthy to carry."

John 1:27 reads, "He who comes after me, the thong of whose sandals I am not worthy to untie."

Mark 1:7 reads, "After me comes he who is mightier than I, the thong of whose sandals I am not worthy to stoop down and untie." Did John—with reference to the sandal—say "not worthy to *carry*" or "not worthy *to untie*" or "not worthy to *stoop down and untie*"?

189. *A Question Concerning the Emergence of the Solar System*
Genesis 1:9-18 reveals that in the Genesis creation scheme the sun, moon, and solar system were created *after* the earth with its vegetation

(fruit-bearing trees and seed-yielding plants). Do scientists believe the earth, apple trees, and tomatoes came into existence *before* the sun, moon, and solar system?

190. *A Question Concerning Esau's Wives*

Esau, a polygamist, married a woman named *Adah* and a woman named *Basemath*. Genesis 36:3 reports that *Basemath* was the daughter of *Ishmael*. Contrarily, Genesis 26:34 reports that Basemath was the daughter of *Elon the Hittite*. Yet curiously, Genesis 36:2 states that Esau's wife named *Adah* was the daughter of *Elon the Hittite*. Which one of Elon's daughters did Esau marry? Did he marry Elon's daughter named *Basemath* (as Genesis 26:34 indicates), or did he marry Elon's daughter named *Adah* (as Genesis 36:2 indicates)? Was *Basemath* the daughter of *Elon the Hittite* (as Genesis 26:34 contends) or was she the daughter of *Ishmael* (as Genesis 36:3 contends)?

Esau also had a wife named *Oholibamah* (Genesis 36:2, 14, 18, 25). Assuming that Oholibamah was Esau's *wife*, why does Genesis 36:41 identify Oholibamah as an Edomite *chieftain*?

191. *A Question Concerning Jacob's Household*

Acts 7:14 reports that 75 kindred (the household of Jacob) went down into Egypt during Joseph's time in order to take advantage of the food supply.

Contrarily, Genesis 46:27 reports that 70 members of Jacob's house went down into Egypt. This tradition is repeated in Exodus 1:5.

Did Jacob's household—at the time of the descent into Egypt—consist of 70 or 75 members? Which figure is correct?

192. *A Question Concerning God's Finger*

Luke 11:14-23 contains an account of the Beelzebul charge leveled against Jesus. In the context of this accusation (according to Luke)

Jesus said, "If it is *by the finger of God* that I cast out demons, then the kingdom of God has come upon you."

Matthew 12:22-29 also contains an account of the Beelzebul charge. In this Matthean account Jesus is reported to have said, "If it is by *the spirit of God* that I cast out demons, then the kingdom of God has come upon you."

Which phrase is correct? Did Jesus say "*by the finger of God*" or "*by the spirit of God*"?

193. *A Question Concerning Disobedient Sons*
Deuteronomy 21:18-21 provides that disobedient sons be stoned to death. Is stoning to death of disobedient sons a commendable practice?

194. *A Question Concerning Body Organs*
Deuteronomy 23:1 decrees that a man with crushed testicles or a severed organ should be excluded from the Lord's assembly. Should a person be excluded from the Lord's assembly because of physical mutilation?

195. *A Question Concerning the Centurion's Observation*
Did the Centurion—at the moment of Jesus' death—remark, "Truly this man was a son of God" (as Matthew 27:54 and Mark 15:39 report), or did the Centurion—at the moment of Jesus' death— remark, "Beyond all doubt, this man was innocent" (as Luke 23:47 reports)?

196. *A Question Concerning Caesarea Philippi*
In Matthew 16:13 Caesarea Philippi is (rightfully) conceived as a city with a surrounding territory. However, in Mark 8:27 Caesarea Philippi is curiously conceived as a territory having villages. Was Caesarea Philippi a city with a territory (as Matthew 16:13 implies) or was it a territory having villages (as Mark 8:27 implies)?

197. *A Question Concerning the Bread at the Last Supper*

Matthew, Mark, Luke, and I Corinthians contain accounts of Jesus' meal with the disciples immediately prior to the crucifixion. At this meal Jesus and the disciples shared bread about which Jesus made an observation. This bread observation is reported in Matthew, Mark, Luke, and I Corinthians as follows:

> "Take this and eat; this is my body" (Matthew 26:26).

> "Take this; this is my body" (Mark 14:22).

> "This is my body" (Luke 22:19).

> "This is my body which is for you; do this as a memorial of me" (I Corinthians 11:24).

These four statements are different from one another. In other words, no two are identical. Which one is the correct report of Jesus' bread observation at the Last Supper?

198. *A Question Concerning the Cup of Wine at the Last Supper*

Matthew, Mark, Luke, and I Corinthians contain accounts of Jesus' meal with the disciples immediately prior to the crucifixion. At this meal Jesus and the disciples shared a cup of wine about which Jesus made an observation. This cup-of-wine observation is reported in Matthew, Mark, Luke, and I Corinthians as follows:

> "Drink from it, all of you. For this is my blood, the blood of the covenant, shed for many for the forgiveness of sins. I tell you, never again shall I drink from the fruit of the vine until that day when I drink it new with you in the Kingdom of my Father" (Matthew 26:28-29).

> "This is my blood, the blood of the covenant, shed for many. I tell you this: Never again shall I drink from the fruit of the vine until that day when I drink it new in the Kingdom of God" (Mark 14:24-25).

"Take this and share it among yourselves; for I tell you, from this moment I shall drink from the fruit of the vine no more until the time when the Kingdom of God comes" (Luke 22:17-18).

"This cup is the new covenant sealed by my blood. Whenever you drink it, do this as a memorial of me" (I Corinthians 11:25).

These four statements are different from one another. In other words, no two are identical. Which one is the correct report of Jesus' cup-of-wine observation at the Last Supper?

199. *A Question Concerning the Levites*
According to Deuteronomy 10:9, Numbers 18:21-24, and Numbers 26:57-62, the Levites were to have no portion of the Promised Land. In other words, the Levites were to be landless. Yet according to Joshua 21:1-42 and I Chronicles 6:54-81, forty-eight cities (along with their surrounding pastures) were to be set apart as dwelling places for the Levites. Which tradition is correct? Were the Levites supposed to be landless, or were they supposed to inherit forty-eight cities with their pasture lands?

200. *A Question Concerning a Circumference*
A contemporary inerrantist's spokesman describes the Bible as "the flawless epitome of impeccable perfection to the minutest, microscopic detail." Does this claim hold in light of the description of the molten sea in Solomon's temple? This molten sea was circular in shape. I Kings 7:23 and II Chronicles 4:2 state that the ratio of the circular sea's diameter to circumference was one to three. This ratio produced the puzzling formula C = 3d. Is this formula correct in view of the well-known geometric formula C = *pi*d?